IMPACT™
SOCIAL STUDIES

Regions of the United States

INQUIRY JOURNAL

Mc
Graw
Hill

Program Authors

James Banks, Ph.D.
University of Washington
Seattle, Washington

Kevin P. Colleary, Ed.D.
Fordham University
New York, New York

William Deverell, Ph.D.
University of Southern California
Los Angeles, California

Daniel Lewis, Ph.D.
The Huntington Library
Los Angeles, California

Elizabeth Logan, Ph.D., J.D.
USC Institute on California and the West
Los Angeles, California

Walter C. Parker, Ph.D.
University of Washington
Seattle, Washington

Emily M. Schell, Ed.D.
San Diego State University
San Diego, California

mheducation.com/prek-12

Send all inquiries to:
McGraw Hill
120 S. Riverside Plaze, Suite 1200
Chicago, IL 60606

ISBN: 978-0-07-691441-8
MHID: 0-07-691441-0

Printed in the United States of America.

8 9 LWI 25 24 23 22

D

Program Consultants

Tahira DuPree Chase, Ed.D.
Greenburgh Central School District
Hartsdale, New York

Jana Echevarria, Ph.D.
California State University
Long Beach, California

Douglas Fisher, Ph.D.
San Diego State University
San Diego, California

Nafees Khan, Ph.D.
Clemson University
Clemson, South Carolina

Jay McTighe
McTighe & Associates Consulting
Columbia, Maryland

Carlos Ulloa, Ed.D.
Escondido Union School District
Escondido, California

Rebecca Valbuena, M.Ed.
Glendora Unified School District
Glendora, California

Program Reviewers

Gary Clayton, Ph.D.
Northern Kentucky University
Highland Heights, Kentucky

Lorri Glover, Ph.D.
Saint Louis University
St. Louis, Missouri

Thomas Herman, Ph.D.
San Diego State University
San Diego, California

Clifford Trafzer, Ph.D.
University of California
Riverside, California

Letter From the Authors

Dear Social Studies Detective,

Think about the region you live in. What state do you live in? What is it like? Then imagine your region long, long ago. Why did different groups of people decide to settle there? What were their experiences over time? In this book you will find out more about the rich and interesting history of all the regions of the United States. You will see firsthand how geography influences the people and culture of our nation and how it helped our country grow!

As you read, take on the role of a detective. You may have questions. Write them down and then analyze the text to find the answers. Take notes—write down what interests you! You can use your notes to share the excitement of our country's history. Look closely—photos of real people and real places will bring these topics to life. Study the maps and read the time lines to see the changes that took place in each state and region across the country.

Enjoy your investigation into the world of social studies where you will find out how people came together to create a diverse and exciting nation. How will you become a responsible and involved citizen? Read on for some ideas!

Sincerely,
The IMPACT Social Studies Authors

Avalon Harbor, Catalina Island, California

Contents

Reference Source

Chapter 1

The Land and People of the United States

 How Does America Use Its Strengths and Face Its Challenges?

Chapter

2

The Northeast

Why Have People Moved To and From the Northeast?

Chapter 3

The Southeast

How Has the Southeast Changed Over Time?

Chapter 4

The Midwest

ESSENTIAL EQ QUESTION

How Does the Midwest Reflect the Spirit of America?

Chapter

5

The Southwest

How Does the Southwest Reflect Its Diverse Past and Unique Environment?

Chapter 6

The West

What Draws People to the West?

Skills and Features

My Notes

_____

_____

_____

_____

_____

_____

_____

_____

_____

Getting Started

You have two social studies books that you will use together to explore and analyze important social studies issues.

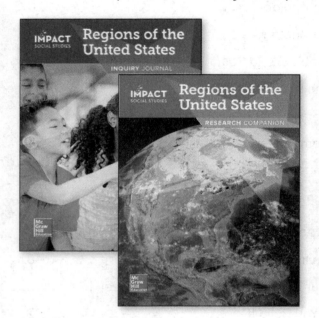

The Inquiry Journal

is your reporter's notebook where you will ask questions, analyze sources, and record information.

The Research Companion

is where you'll read nonfiction and literature selections, examine primary source materials, and look for answers to your questions.

Every Chapter

Chapter opener pages help you see the big picture. Each chapter begins with an **Essential Question**. This **EQ** guides research and inquiry.

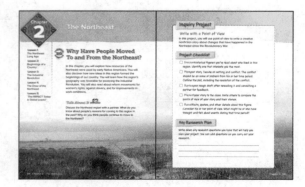

In the **Inquiry Journal,** you'll talk about the **EQ** and find out about the EQ Inquiry Project for the chapter.

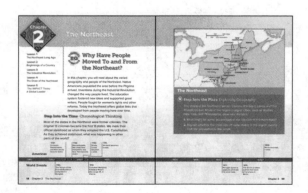

In the **Research Companion**, you'll explore the **EQ** and use a time line and map to establish the lesson's time and place.

Explore Words

Find out what you know about the chapter's academic and domain-specific vocabulary.

Explore Words

Complete this chapter's Word Rater. Write notes as you learn more about each word.

abolitionist — My Notes
☐ Know It!
☐ Heard It!
☐ Don't Know It!

charter — My Notes
☐ Know It!
☐ Heard It!
☐ Don't Know It!

industrialization — My Notes
☐ Know It!
☐ Heard It!
☐ Don't Know It!

negotiate — My Notes
☐ Know It!
☐ Heard It!
☐ Don't Know It!

protest — My Notes
☐ Know It!
☐ Heard It!
☐ Don't Know It!

quarry — My Notes
☐ Know It!
☐ Heard It!
☐ Don't Know It!

raw material — My Notes
☐ Know It!
☐ Heard It!
☐ Don't Know It!

revolutionary — My Notes
☐ Know It!
☐ Heard It!
☐ Don't Know It!

suffrage — My Notes
☐ Know It!
☐ Heard It!
☐ Don't Know It!

waterway — My Notes
☐ Know It!
☐ Heard It!
☐ Don't Know It!

56 Chapter 2 The Northeast

Chapter 2 57

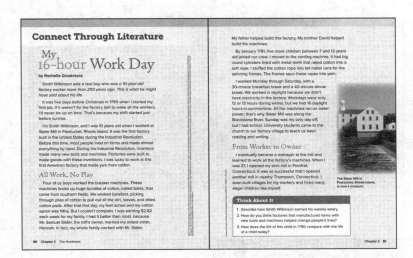

Connect Through Literature

My 16-hour Work Day
by Rochelle Groskreutz

Smith Wilkinson was a real boy who was a 10-year-old factory worker more than 200 years ago. This is what he might have said about his life.

It was five days before Christmas in 1790 when I started my first job. If it weren't for the factory bell to wake all the workers, I'd never be up on time. That's because my shift started just before sunrise.

I'm Smith Wilkinson, and I was 10 years old when I worked at Slater Mill in Pawtucket, Rhode Island. It was the first factory built in the United States during the Industrial Revolution. Before this time, most people lived on farms and made almost everything by hand. During the Industrial Revolution, inventors made many new tools and machines. Factories were built to make goods with these inventions. I was lucky to work at this first American factory that made yarn from cotton.

All Work, No Play

Four of us boys worked the breaker machines. These machines broke up huge bundles of cotton, called bales, that came from southern fields. We worked barefoot, picking through piles of cotton to pull out all the dirt, leaves, and dried cotton pods. After that first day, my feet ached and my cotton apron was filthy. But I couldn't complain. I was earning $2.82 each week for my family. I had it better than most, because Mr. Samuel Slater, the mill's owner, married my oldest sister, Hannah. In fact, my whole family worked with Mr. Slater.

My father helped build this factory. My brother David helped build the machines.

By January 1791, five more children between 7 and 12 years old joined our crew. I moved to the carding machine. It had big round cylinders lined with metal teeth that raked cotton into a soft rope. I stuffed the cotton rope into tall metal cans for the spinning frames. The frames spun these ropes into yarn.

I worked Monday through Saturday, with a 30-minute breakfast break and a 40-minute dinner break. We worked in daylight because we didn't have electricity in the factory. Workdays were only 12 or 13 hours during winter, but we had 16 daylight hours in summertime. All the machines ran on water power; that's why Slater Mill was along the Blackstone River. Sunday was my only day off, but I had school. University students came to the church in our factory village to teach us basic reading and writing.

From Worker to Owner

I eventually became a manager at the mill and learned to work all the factory's machines. When I was 27, I opened my own mill in Pomfret, Connecticut. It was so successful that I opened another mill in nearby Thompson, Connecticut. I even built villages for my workers and hired many eager children like myself.

The Slater Mill in Pawtucket, Rhode Island, is now a museum.

Think About It

1. Describe how Smith Wilkinson earned his weekly salary.
2. How do you think factories that manufactured items with new tools and machines helped change people's lives?
3. How does the life of this child in 1790 compare with the life of a child today?

60 Chapter 2 The Northeast

Chapter 2 61

Connect Through Literature

Explore the chapter topic through fiction, informational text, and poetry.

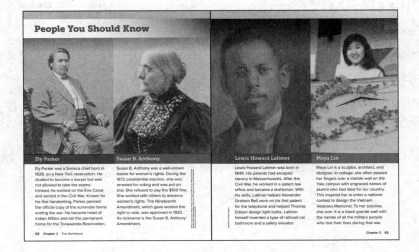

People You Should Know

Ely Parker
Ely Parker was a Seneca chief born in 1828, on a New York reservation. He studied to become a lawyer but was not allowed to take the exams. Instead, he worked on the Erie Canal and served in the Civil War. Known for his fine handwriting, Parker penned the official copy of the surrender terms ending the war. He became head of Indian Affairs and set the permanent home for the Tonawanda Reservation.

Susan B. Anthony
Susan B. Anthony was a well-known leader for women's rights. During the 1872 presidential election, she was arrested for voting and was put on trial. She refused to pay the $100 fine. She worked with others to advance women's rights. The Nineteenth Amendment, which gave women the right to vote, was approved in 1920. Its nickname is the Susan B. Anthony Amendment.

Lewis Howard Latimer
Lewis Howard Latimer was born in 1848. His parents had escaped slavery in Massachusetts. After the Civil War, he worked in a patent law office and became a draftsman. With his skills, Latimer helped Alexander Graham Bell work on his first patent for the telephone and helped Thomas Edison design light bulbs. Latimer himself invented a type of railroad car bathroom and a safety elevator.

Maya Lin
Maya Lin is a sculptor, architect, and designer. In college, she often passed her fingers over a marble wall on the Yale campus with engraved names of alumni who had died for our country. This inspired her to enter a national contest to design the Vietnam Veterans Memorial. To her surprise, she won. It is a black granite wall with the names of all the military people who lost their lives during that war.

62 Chapter 2 The Northeast

Chapter 2 63

People You Should Know

Learn about the lives of people who have made an impact in history.

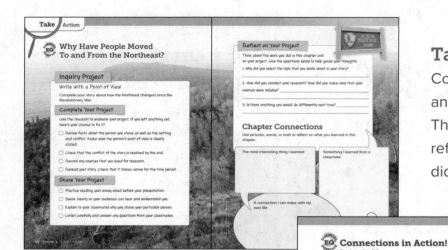

Take Action

Complete your Inquiry Project and share it with your class. Then take time to discuss and reflect on your project. What did you learn?

Connections in Action

Think about the people, places, and events you read about in the chapter. Discuss with a partner how this gives you a deeper understanding of the EQ.

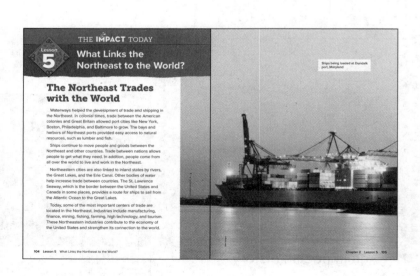

The IMPACT Today

Take what you have learned about the chapter's region and tie it to the world. Consider how key questions related to geography, economics, and citizenship connect each region to the world.

Every Lesson

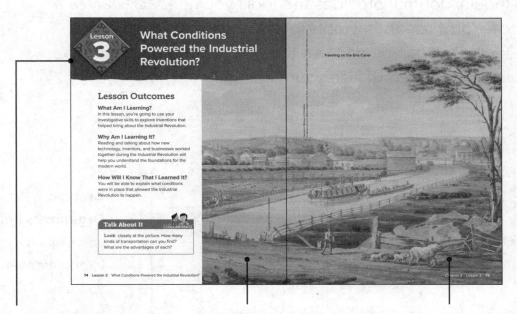

Lesson Question lets you think about how the lesson connects to the chapter EQ.

Lesson Outcomes help you think about what you will be learning and how it applies to the EQ.

Images and text provide opportunities to explore the lesson topic.

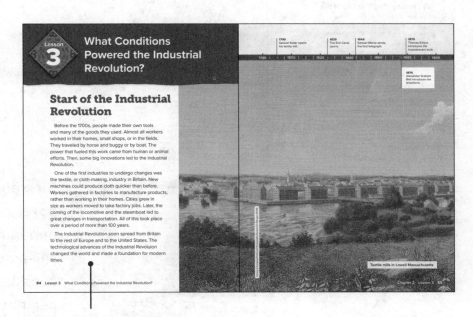

Lesson selections deepen your understanding of the lesson topic and its connection to the EQ.

Analyze and Inquire

The Inquiry Journal provides the tools you need to analyze a source. You'll use those tools to investigate the texts in the Research Companion and use the graphic organizer in the Inquiry Journal to organize your findings.

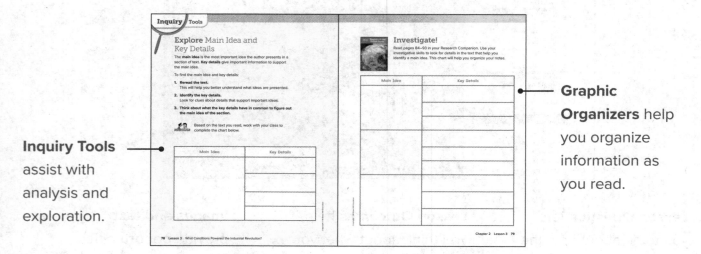

Inquiry Tools assist with analysis and exploration.

Graphic Organizers help you organize information as you read.

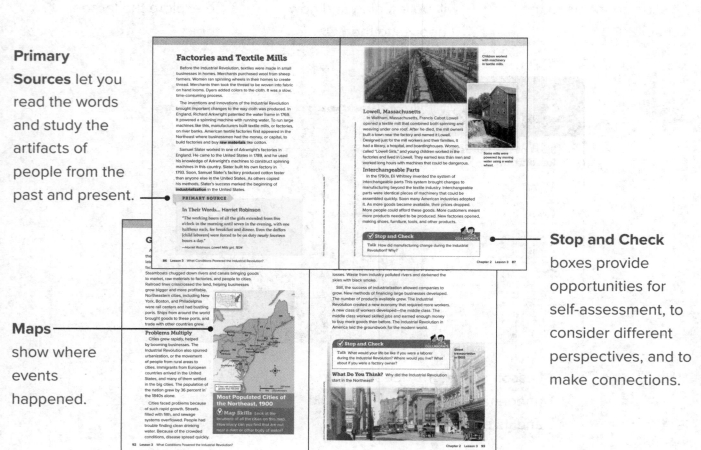

Primary Sources let you read the words and study the artifacts of people from the past and present.

Stop and Check boxes provide opportunities for self-assessment, to consider different perspectives, and to make connections.

Maps show where events happened.

Report Your Findings

At the end of each lesson, you have an opportunity in the Inquiry Journal to report your findings and connect back to the EQ. In the Research Companion, you'll reconsider the lesson focus question based on what you've learned.

Think about what you have learned.

Write About It using text evidence to support your ideas.

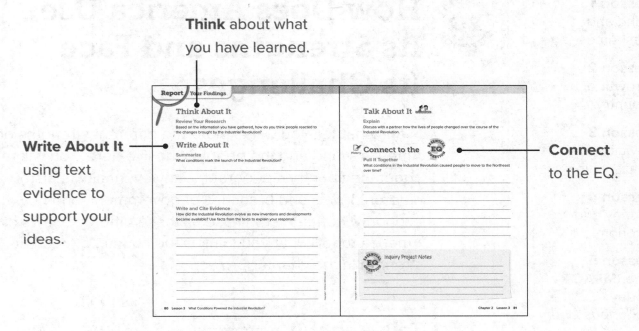

Connect to the EQ.

Think about what you read in the lesson. How does this give you a new understanding about the lesson focus question?

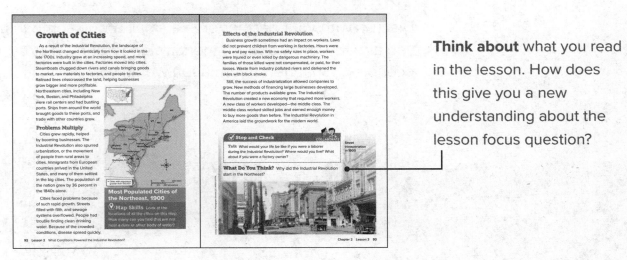

Chapter 1

The Land and People of the United States

ESSENTIAL EQ QUESTION

How Does America Use Its Strengths and Face Its Challenges?

In this chapter, you will explore the different strengths of America's land and the people who live here. You will read about the country's geography, key events in its history, different levels and branches of government, and how the economy works. You will use all these different views of America to tell what you think is the country's greatest strength in the chapter project.

Talk About It

Discuss with your partner or in a small group some things you already know about America's geography, history, or economy. What new information would you like to learn?

Inquiry Project

Make an Advertisement for America

What is America's greatest strength? Is it our geography, history, government, economy, or people? Choose one strength and make an advertisement promoting it using evidence and facts.

Project Checklist

☐ **Select** a topic that you think is America's greatest strength. Brainstorm reasons why you think so.

☐ **Gather** evidence to support your opinion. Consider ways to use these facts to persuade your audience.

☐ **Choose** images to include. Think of ways to make your advertisment eye-catching, as well as informative.

☐ **Draft** a copy of your advertisement to make sure you use facts and evidence to persuade your audience that the strength you chose is America's greatest strength.

☐ **Revise** your advertisement on your own or with a partner. Check that it reflects details you researched, has strong images, and is free of spelling and grammar mistakes.

☐ **Review** your advertisement with a partner and receive their feedback.

My Research Plan

Write down any research questions you have that will help you plan your project. You can add questions as you carry out your research.

_____

_____

_____

Complete this chapter's Word Rater.
Write notes as you learn more about each word.

amendment

☐ Know It!
☐ Heard It!
☐ Don't Know It!

My Notes

_____

_____

_____

colonist

☐ Know It!
☐ Heard It!
☐ Don't Know It!

My Notes

_____

_____

_____

democracy

☐ Know It!
☐ Heard It!
☐ Don't Know It!

My Notes

_____

_____

_____

ethnic

☐ Know It!
☐ Heard It!
☐ Don't Know It!

My Notes

_____

_____

_____

expansion

☐ Know It!
☐ Heard It!
☐ Don't Know It!

My Notes

_____

_____

_____

immigrant

My Notes

☐ Know It!

☐ Heard It!

☐ Don't Know It!

_____

_____

_____

import

My Notes

☐ Know It!

☐ Heard It!

☐ Don't Know It!

_____

_____

_____

latitude

My Notes

☐ Know It!

☐ Heard It!

☐ Don't Know It!

_____

_____

_____

longitude

My Notes

☐ Know It!

☐ Heard It!

☐ Don't Know It!

_____

_____

_____

scarcity

My Notes

☐ Know It!

☐ Heard It!

☐ Don't Know It!

_____

_____

_____

Lesson 1

How Does Geography Define a Region?

Lesson Outcomes

What Am I Learning?

In this lesson, you're going to use your investigative skills to identify important features of maps and geographic features of the United States.

Why Am I Learning It?

Reading and talking about maps and geographic features will help you learn more about the unique features of the United States.

How Will I Know That I Learned It?

You will be able to recognize maps as representations of Earth, identify map features, and describe features geographers use to analyze different locations.

Talk About It

Look closely at the image. What part of Earth does it show? How do you know? What geographic features do you recognize in the image?

A satellite image of Earth from NASA

1 Inspect

Look Inspect the map and read the text. What do you think it shows?

Circle details in the map that help you understand how to use it.

Identify clues that tell you:

- How are the lines of latitude and longitude used?
- What features of the area in the map are labeled?
- How are directions in the map shown?

My Notes

_____

_____

_____

_____

_____

_____

_____

_____

Pointing It Out with Latitude and Longitude

This is a map of North America. It shows lines of **latitude** and **longitude**. Latitude lines run side to side. Longitude lines run top to bottom. These lines are the same on every map. Geographers use them to locate a place on Earth.

To identify an exact location on the map, find the point where the two lines meet. You can name this point with a set of numbers called coordinates. The latitude line is written first. Then the longitude line is written second. We write the numbers in degrees, using the ° symbol.

As an example, look for the point where the 30° line of latitude intersects the 90° line of longitude. What city is labeled near that coordinate? The coordinates for New Orleans are written as 30°N, 90°W. Using coordinates is one way to find the absolute location of a place on a map.

Geographers also use the compass rose to identify one location relative to another. The compass rose indicates the four directions: north, south, east, and west. For example, Phoenix, Arizona, is south of Salt Lake City, Utah.

The map scale shows the distance between two points on the map in relation to the actual distance on Earth. According to the scale, Phoenix is about 600 miles from Salt Lake City.

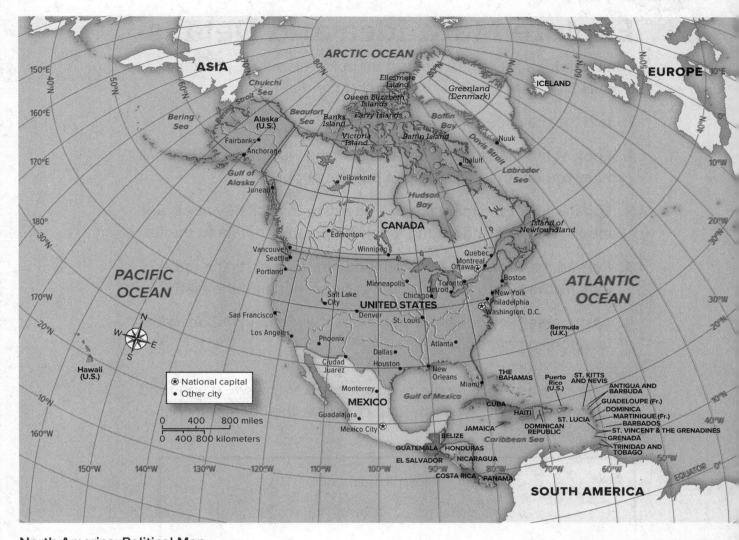

North America: Political Map

2 Find Evidence

Look Again Why do you think latitude and longitude have been helpful to geographers?

Highlight the lines of latitude and longitude that pass through the United States.

3 Make Connections

Talk How can you use latitude and longitude to identify a specific location? Find Denver, Colorado, on the map. How would you describe the location of Denver using latitude and longitude coordinates?

COLLABORATE

Explore Main Idea and Details

The **main idea** is the most important point the author presents.
Details are the key points that support the main idea.

To find the main idea:

1. Look at the map and read the text all the way through. This will help you understand what the page is about.

2. Look again at the map and pay attention to all the symbols and labels. Do the symbols and labels help you understand the text?

3. Reread the text. Look for information that supports the main idea. Is there a connection between the map and the text?

4. Ask yourself, *What information helps me identify and describe locations on a map?*

 Based on the map you analyzed and the text you read, work with your class to complete the chart below.

Main Idea

↓

Detail

Investigate!

Read pages 8–17 in your Research Companion. Use your investigative skills to look for text evidence that provides details to support the main idea. This chart will help you organize your notes.

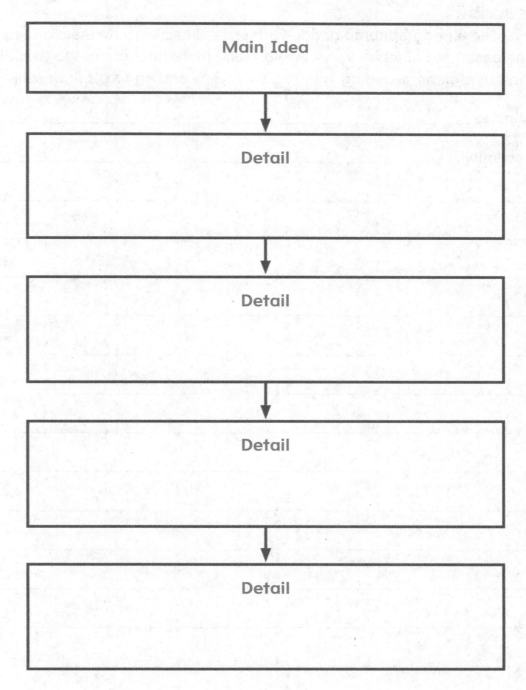

Main Idea

Detail

Detail

Detail

Detail

Think About It

Review your research. Based on the information you have gathered, what different ways can you use geography to describe a location or region?

Write About It

Describe

Think like a geographer to define your state. Describe your state and its location in at least three different ways. As you read more throughout the year about different regions, including your region, review and add to your description.

My state: _____

Description _____

_____

_____

_____

_____

_____

_____

_____

_____

_____

_____

Talk About It

Compare

Share your descriptions with a partner. Do you have similar information? Compare and add any new information to your description.

 ography

Connect to the

Create a Poster

Create a poster to attract tourists to your state based on key geographical features. Then write a paragraph describing how your state contributes to the strength of the United States.

_____

_____

_____

_____

_____

_____

Inquiry Project Notes

_____

_____

_____

_____

_____

Lesson 2

How Has America Stayed United Through Growth and Challenges?

Lesson Outcomes

What Am I Learning?

In this lesson, you are going to use your investigative skills to explore what changes and challenges America experienced as it grew into the nation it is today.

Why Am I Learning It?

Reading and talking about important events in America's history will help you understand how the nation grew.

How Will I Know That I Learned It?

You will be able to explain the challenges that helped shape America and how our nation grew from these events.

Talk About It

COLLABORATE

Look closely at the picture of Chicago, Illinois. What is happening in this picture? What might the people in Chicago be celebrating?

Chicago, Illinois

Declaring Independence

1 Inspect

Read Look at the title. What do you think this text will be about?

Circle words you don't know.

Underline clues that tell you:

- Who was involved in this event?
- When did it happen?
- What was the purpose of this event?

My Notes

_____

_____

_____

_____

_____

_____

_____

_____

Before the United States became a nation, it was a collection of thirteen separate colonies. The colonies were ruled by the British king, George III. Under the king, American **colonists** did not have the same rights as people living in Great Britain. They had no say in what laws the British government chose to make about how they lived or traded. They knew this was unfair. The colonists wanted to declare their freedom from British rule.

In May of 1775, after the American Revolution had begun, each colony sent representatives to meet in the city of Philadelphia. They called themselves the Second Continental Congress. The members of this Congress agreed they should unite the colonies and govern themselves. After voting to form an independent nation, the Congress decided to send out a document explaining its decision. In 1776, a committee of five men wrote the Declaration of Independence. Their names were Thomas Jefferson, John Adams, Benjamin Franklin, Roger Sherman, and Robert Livingston.

The writers of the Declaration of Independence created several drafts that were edited and revised by members of the Congress.

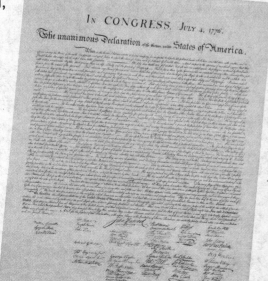

In Their Words... Thomas Jefferson

"We hold these truths to be self-evident, that all men are created equal, that they are endowed by their Creator with certain unalienable rights, that among these are life, liberty and the pursuit of happiness."

—Included in the Declaration of Independence, July 1776

Signing the Declaration of Independence.

The final document was approved by the Congress on July 4, 1776. The members of the Congress signed their names at the bottom in support of the agreement. The Declaration of Independence announced to the world that the American colonists were a free and separate people, ready to govern themselves.

But, before the colonists could truly govern themselves, there was a war to be won.

2 Find Evidence

Reread What do you think the words "life," "liberty," and "pursuit of happiness" included in the Declaration of Independence mean?

Highlight examples of the unfair treatment the people in the colonies were experiencing.

3 Make Connections

Talk
Think about the writers of the Declaration of Independence. What message did they want to send?

COLLABORATE

Explore Cause and Effect

The **cause** is why something happened.

The **effect** is the result of what happened.

To find the cause and effect:

1. Read the text all the way through.

2. Reread the text and look for something that tells you what happened. This is the effect.

3. Reread the text again and look for a detail that tells you why it happened. This is the cause.

4. Ask yourself, *Did the cause directly lead to the event that happened?*

 Based on the text you read, work with your class to complete the chart below.

Cause Why Something Happened	Effect The Result

Investigate!

Read pages 18–27 in your Research Companion. Use your investigative skills to look for text evidence that tells you what happened and why it happened. This chart will help you organize your notes.

Cause Why Something Happened	Effect The Result

Think About It

Review your research. Based on the information you have gathered, how do you think America has stayed united throughout its history?

Write About It

Write and Cite Evidence

Think about important events or challenges that happened in American history from the text or your own research. Choose one event you think is the most important in American history. Tell what caused the event, what happened in the event, and the effect the event had on the United States as a nation.

_____

_____

_____

_____

_____

_____

_____

_____

_____

_____

_____

Talk About It

Compare Your Analysis

Discuss which event you think was most important to the United States and why with a partner. If your event was different, what similarities did the events have? If your event was the same, how were your explanations of causes and effects different?

Connect to the

Pull It Together

Using what you've learned in this lesson, how do you think America has become a stronger nation through the challenges it faced throughout our history?

_____

_____

_____

_____

_____

Inquiry Project Notes

_____

_____

_____

_____

_____

Lesson 3

How Does the Structure of Our Government Work?

Lesson Outcomes

What Am I Learning?
In this lesson, you're going to use your investigative skills to explore the powers that belong to the federal, state, and local governments.

Why Am I Learning It?
Reading and talking about the levels of government will help you learn how federal, state, and local governments work together to serve the people of the nation.

How Will I Know That I Learned It?
You will be able to explain the purpose of the United States Constitution and the powers held by federal, state, and local governments.

Talk About It
COLLABORATE

Look closely at the picture. Who are these people? What do you think they are doing? How do you know?

Scene at the Signing of the Constitution of the United States, an oil painting by Howard Chandler Christy, hangs in the United States Capitol.

Creating the Constitution

Read Look at the title. What do you think this text will be about?

Circle words you don't know.

Underline clues that answer these questions:

- **Who** attended the Constitutional Convention?
- **What** happened at the Constitutional Convention?
- **How** was the United States Constitution made into law?

My Notes

_____

_____

_____

_____

_____

_____

_____

_____

_____

_____

In 1787, the United States was still a new country. It declared its independence from Great Britain just eleven years earlier. The young nation faced dangers from foreign countries and challenges within its states. Leaders had to decide what role the national government should have in solving the country's problems. So, in 1787, state leaders met in Philadelphia, Pennsylvania, to decide how the country should be governed.

This meeting was called the Constitutional Convention. It lasted from May 14th to September 17th. The delegates discussed important questions facing the nation. What powers should the national government have? How should the government be organized to best serve the people?

The delegates had heated debates. On July 24, a few delegates were chosen to write a document that would outline the powers and structure of the national government. This document became the first draft of the United States Constitution.

PRIMARY SOURCE

In Their Words... John Dickinson

"Let our government be like that of the solar system. Let the general government be like the sun and the states the planets, repelled yet attracted, and the whole moving regularly and harmoniously in several orbits."

—John Dickinson, Delaware Delegate, 1787

Copyright © McGraw-Hill Education
TEXT: Dickinson, John. Speaking before the Constitutional Convention, June 4, 1787.

The United States Constitution became the law of the nation in 1788.

When the draft was finished, all of the delegates discussed the new Constitution. They held debates on slavery, population, and state representation. On September 17, 1787, most of the delegates approved the document. It was then sent to the states.

For the Constitution to become law, nine of the thirteen states had to ratify, or approve it. People throughout the country debated the Constitution. Some people supported it because it separated the power of the national government. Others believed it gave too much power to the national government. They wanted to make sure that the Constitution did not limit state or local government powers.

Delaware was the first state to approve the Constitution on December 7, 1787. Over time, more states ratified it. Finally, on June 21, 1788, New Hampshire became the ninth state to officially approve the Constitution. From that day forward, the Constitution became the law of the nation.

2 Find Evidence

Reread Why was there disagreement on the power that the national government should have? What details did the author include about people's opinions?

How does the quotation by John Dickinson relate to the information in the text? What words and phrases does Dickinson use to describe how the government should be like the solar system?

3 Make Connections

Talk Discuss with a partner why the Constitution was an important document for the United States. What details in the text support your answer?

COLLABORATE

Inquiry Tools

Explore Compare and Contrast

When you compare and contrast, you explain how two or more things are alike and different. Comparing and contrasting helps you identify similarities and differences among events and ideas.

1. **Read the text once all the way through.**
    This will help you understand what the text is about.

2. **Look for key facts and details that show differences about similar topics.**
    How are the topics different? Which facts and details show these differences?

3. **Look for key facts and details that show similarities about the topics.**
    How are the topics the same? Which facts and details show these similarities?

4. **Use key facts or details to compare and contrast the topics.**
    Use important facts and details to explain how the topics are alike and how they are different.

 Based on the text you read, work with your class to complete the chart below.

Approving the Constitution	
Supporters of the Constitution	**People Against the Constitution**

Investigate!

Read pages 28–37 in your Research Companion. Use your investigative skills to identify the similarities and differences among federal, state, and local governments. Use the chart to organize information.

Levels of Government		
Federal Government	**State Government**	**Local Government**

Think About It

Sum Up

Review your research. Based on the information you have gathered, how do federal, state, and local governments share power and responsibilities?

Write About It

Explain

Imagine that you were at the Constitutional Convention. Write a letter to your family that explains the purpose of the Constitution and the powers of federal, state, and local governments.

_____

_____

_____

_____

_____

_____

_____

_____

_____

_____

_____

_____

_____

_____

_____

_____

_____

Talk About It

Take a Stand

With a partner, discuss how the powers of the federal government are alike and different from the powers of the state government. Identify and discuss the reasons and evidence your partner gives to support his or her position.

Civics

Connect to the

Pull It Together

How does the way our government is structured contribute to the strength of America?

_____

_____

_____

_____

_____

_____

Inquiry Project Notes

_____

_____

_____

_____

_____

Lesson 4

How Does Our Economy Work?

Lesson Outcomes

What Am I Learning?

In this lesson, you're going to use your investigative skills to explore what economics is and how the economy affects individuals and nations.

Why Am I Learning It?

Reading and talking about the way the economy functions will help you understand your current and future role in the economy.

How Will I Know That I Learned It?

You will be able to explain what elements make up the economy and how these elements function together.

Talk About It

COLLABORATE

Look closely at the photograph. What is shown? What are the values of the different bills? Why do you think U.S. bills are shown in a lesson about economy?

A Market Economy

Money plays a key role in an economy. People and businesses use money as a tool in a market economy, also called a free market. Companies use money to produce goods and provide services to consumers. Consumers use money to buy products and services. The government plays a limited role in a market economy by setting taxes, printing money, and setting some work and business rules.

In a market economy, businesses and individuals are linked together. Businesses make goods and services to sell to individuals. Individuals provide labor, or work, to businesses.

Money flows between businesses and individuals. Businesses pay workers to produce goods and services. Individuals earn income and use this money to buy goods and services. Businesses make income from selling goods. This is called the circular flow of money.

Money plays a key role in an economy.

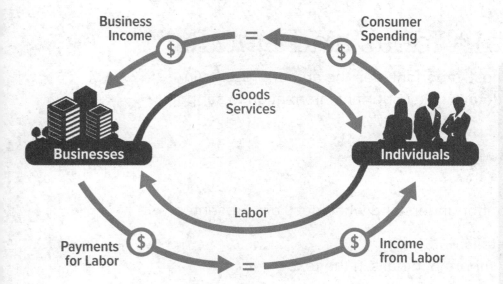

Supply and demand drives prices in a market economy. Supply refers to how much of a certain product is available. Demand is how much people want a product or service. Products in high demand and low supply will have a higher price than those with high supply and low demand.

Demand increases when there are more people in a market and when they have more money to spend. Demand decreases if customers no longer want a product. Supply increases when more sellers start to sell a product or when production of the product is increased. Supply decreases when costs for making the product go up or when the resources needed to create it are not easily available.

The price of a good or service is linked to supply and demand. Companies can compete with each other by offering the same or similar products for lower prices. Lower prices can, in turn, increase demand for a product, while higher prices can decrease demand. Companies try to make higher profits by limiting costs, creating products and services customers want, and setting the best prices based on demand and competition.

2 Find Evidence

Decide Are you willing to pay more for certain products? Why or why not?

Highlight what affects prices of the products people buy.

3 Make Connections

Talk Discuss with a partner COLLABORATE why the price of a product might be higher than the price of another product.

Explore Main Ideas and Details

The **main idea** is the most important idea the author presents in a section of text. **Key details** give important information to support the main idea.

To find the main ideas and details:

1. **Reread the text.**
    This will help you better understand what ideas are presented.

2. **Identify the key details.**
    Look for clues and important details in the text.

3. **Think about what the key details have in common.**
    Connecting how details are related will help you figure out the main idea of the section.

4. **Summarize the main ideas.**
    Write a sentence that summarizes the main idea of each section.

 Based on the text you read, work with your class to complete the web below.

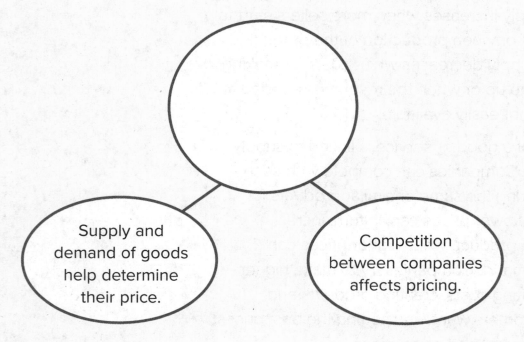

Supply and demand of goods help determine their price.

Competition between companies affects pricing.

Investigate!

Read pages 38–47 in your Research Companion. Use your investigative skills to look for text evidence that tells you the main ideas and key details of the text. This web will help you organize your notes.

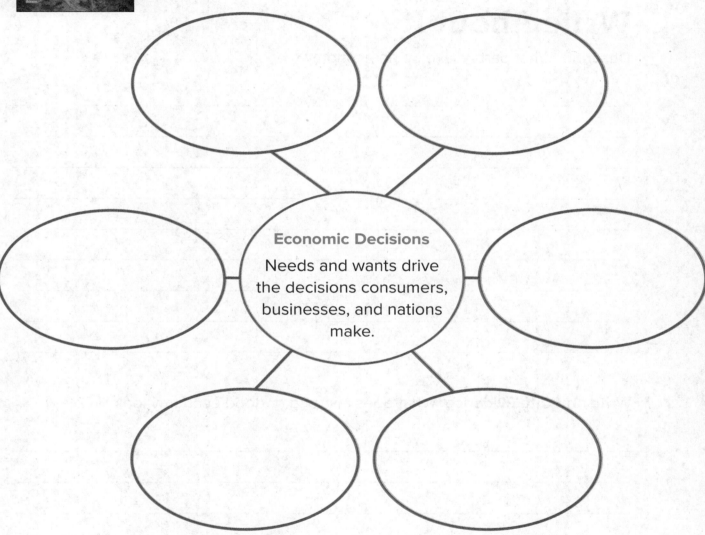

Economic Decisions

Needs and wants drive the decisions consumers, businesses, and nations make.

Think About It

Sum Up

Review your research. Based on the information you have gathered, what are examples of economic choices you can make?

Write About It

Describe What parts make up an economy?

_____

_____

_____

_____

_____

_____

_____

Write and Cite Evidence What does a strong or good economy look like?

_____

_____

_____

_____

_____

_____

_____

Talk About It

Explain

In a small group, brainstorm ideas about how the economy affects individuals and nations. Then, discuss reasons for these effects.

Connect to the

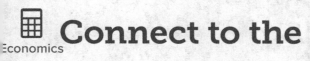

Pull It Together

Think about the information you learned about economics. How does a strong or weak economy affect America and its future?

_____

_____

_____

_____

_____

_____

_____

_____

Inquiry Project Notes

_____

_____

_____

_____

_____

Lesson 5

How Do People of Different Backgrounds Come Together to Form Our Country?

Lesson Outcomes

What Am I Learning?

In this lesson, you're going to use your investigative skills to explore how people of different backgrounds come together to form one country.

Why Am I Learning It?

Reading and talking about different groups of people will help you learn about the diverse cultures that shaped the United States.

How Will I Know That I Learned It?

You will be able to describe the impact people from different backgrounds have had on the United States.

Talk About It

COLLABORATE

Look closely at the picture. What is this statue? What is the statue a symbol of?

Welcoming Immigrants

1 Inspect

Read the title. What do you think you'll learn from this text?

Circle words you want to learn more about.

Underline clues that tell you:

- Where do immigrants come from?
- What impacts do immigrants have?
- What struggles do immigrants have?

My Notes

_____
_____
_____
_____
_____
_____
_____
_____
_____
_____
_____
_____
_____
_____

The United States has a history of **immigrants** coming from different countries at different times. Immigrants have come to America for a variety of reasons. They may have looked to escape hardships in their home country or to find new opportunities America offers. New immigrants bring different cultures to the community.

Throughout America's history, groups of immigrants have formed their own communities and neighborhoods to help keep alive customs from their native or home countries. These communities allow people from different backgrounds to experience the foods, customs, and celebrations of people from all over the world.

America has a mixed history with welcoming immigrants. They have not always been accepted by all communities. Some people dislike or distrust immigrants because they think they are different. This is called prejudice and it has been around from the early years of America, and it continues today.

Ellis Island was the point of entry for many immigrants in the 1900s.

The poem, *The New Colossus*, can be found on a plaque on the inside wall of the base of the Statue of Liberty. The poem gives a message of hope and welcome to immigrants coming to the United States.

PRIMARY SOURCE

The New Colossus

Not like the brazen giant of Greek fame,

With conquering limbs astride from land to land;

Here at our sea-washed, sunset gates shall stand

A mighty woman with a torch, whose flame

Is the imprisoned lightning, and her name

Mother of Exiles. From her beacon-hand

Glows world-wide welcome; her mild eyes command

The air-bridged harbor that twin cities frame.

"Keep, ancient lands, your storied pomp!" cries she

With silent lips. "Give me your tired, your poor,

Your huddled masses yearning to breathe free,

The wretched refuse of your teeming shore.

Send these, the homeless, tempest-tost to me,

I lift my lamp beside the golden door!"

—Poem by Emma Lazarus, originally set at the foot of the Statue of Liberty

Copyright © McGraw-Hill Education
TEXT: Lazarus, Emma. 1883. "The New Colossus." Catalogue of the Pedestal Fund Art Loan Exhibition. New York: National Academy of Design.

2 Find Evidence

Reread What details did the author include to help you learn about how immigrants have impacted communities?

Underline According to *The New Colossus*, who should America accept as immigrants?

3 Make Connections

Think In what ways have immigrants added to your community?

Explore Making Inferences

Making inferences means using text evidence or clues in the text to draw conclusions that the author might not state directly. Readers can apply what they already know about a topic to the evidence or clues in a text to figure out information that is not stated directly.

1. **Read the text once all the way through.**
   This will help you understand what the text is about.

2. **Look at the clues or evidence that are in the text.**
   What facts, data, or details does the author provide about the topic?

3. **Add knowledge you already have that relates to these clues.**
   What are some things you already know that you can connect to this information?

4. **Think about the connections between your prior knowledge and evidence in the text.**
   What can you infer, based on the evidence and what you already know?

Based on the text you read, work with your class to complete the chart below.

Text Clues	What You Know	Inferences
"Give me your tired, your poor, Your huddled masses yearning to breathe free, …"		

Investigate!

Read pages 48–55 in your Research Companion. Use your investigative skills to look for text evidence that helps you make inferences about the impacts immigrants have had on the United States.

Text Clues	What You Know	Inferences
Most Americans are immigrants or descendants of immigrants.		
Each state, city, community, and family may have a different heritage in addition to their American culture.		
Everyone in the United States can celebrate our country no matter what their heritage is or what country they originally come from.		

Think About It

Review Your Research

Based on the information you have gathered, what are different ways people celebrate their own histories and backgrounds as well as America's history?

Write About It

Write and Cite Evidence

How can people honor their specific heritage and come together with people from different backgrounds to form a strong community? Use examples from the texts to explain your response.

_____

_____

_____

_____

_____

_____

_____

_____

_____

_____

_____

_____

_____

_____

Talk About It

Explain
Share your response with a small group. Together, discuss different ways people from diverse backgrounds celebrate their heritage and come together to form a united community.

Connect to the

Pull It Together
How is diversity of people important to life in the United States?

_____

_____

_____

_____

_____

_____

_____

Inquiry Project Notes

_____

_____

_____

_____

_____

Take Action

ESSENTIAL EQ QUESTION

How Does America Use Its Strengths and Face Its Challenges?

Inquiry Project

Make an Advertisement for America

Now complete your advertisement using a checklist, and then share it with the class.

Complete Your Project

Use the checklist to evaluate your advertisement.

☐ Review your topic. Be sure that your idea makes sense.

☐ Check that you have enough details to support your idea.

☐ Record any sources that you used for research.

☐ Make sure your advertisement promotes what you think is America's greatest strength.

Share Your Project

☐ Before you share your advertisement with the class, rehearse your presentation.

☐ Explain to the class why you chose your topic.

☐ Answer any questions from your classmates.

☐ Discuss any points with those who have different opinions.

Inquiry Process Reflection

Think about the work you did in this chapter and on your project. Use the questions below to help guide your thoughts.

1. Why did you choose the topic that you researched?

_____

2. How did you conduct your research? Is there anything you would do differently next time? _____

_____

3. How did you make sure that your sources were reliable? _____

_____

Chapter Connections

Use pictures, words, or both to reflect on what you learned in this chapter.

The most interesting thing I learned:

Something I learned from a classmate:

A connection I can make with my own life:

An International Day to Remember

CHARACTERS

Narrator	Mr. Lee	Miguel
Ronit	Jana	Ms. Franklin
Chorus	Rick	
Carl	Mei	

Narrator: It was Thursday in Oak Valley School.

Chorus: Oak Valley School? Where's that?

Narrator: It's located in a community in California. All over the valley, there are majestic oak trees. Above the valley, there are rugged mountains. And beyond the mountains to the west, you can see—

Chorus: The Pacific Ocean!

Narrator: That's right. Over time, this once small town had grown into a city as families moved here from across the United States and around the world.

Chorus: They helped make Oak Valley what it is today.

Narrator: That's right. Well, on one particular Thursday, the weather in Oak Valley was sunny, but the mood in Mr. Lee's fourth grade classroom was gloomy.

Chorus: Oh, no! What happened?

Narrator: Mr. Lee's class was supposed to go on a field trip to the Cultural Center. They were going to take part in an International Day.

Chorus: Sounds interesting! Um, what *is* an International Day?

Narrator: It's a day that celebrates all the cultures that make our region such a great place to live.

Chorus: That's wonderful!

Narrator: But they did not go.

Chorus: That's terrible! What happened?

Narrator: The bus broke down, and Mr. Lee could not get another bus in time.

Chorus: What happened next?

Narrator: Come see for yourself. This is Mr. Lee's classroom, and here are his students.

Chorus: They sure look disappointed.

Narrator: They do. If only someone had an idea.

Rick: *(raises his hand)* Mr. Lee?

Mr. Lee: Yes, Rick?

Rick: I have an idea.

Chorus: Yay!

Narrator: Ssh! You don't even know what it is yet.

Rick: Since we can't go to International Day, what if International Day comes to us?

Ronit: Oh, I see! We could hold our own International Day at Oak Valley School!

Mei: Oh, could we, Mr. Lee? After all, we have so many different cultures right here in our own city. We could celebrate with traditional food. I can bring Chinese noodles.

Carl: Good idea! I can ask my parents to help me make some traditional Caribbean dishes.

Jana: Like cornmeal dumplings and fresh papaya.

Ronit: I know how to make *challah* bread from Israel.

Miguel: Well, I make the best Mexican salsa.

Mr. Lee: Wow! Perhaps we could do our own International Day. But can we also come up with some activities? After all, food is just one part of cultural traditions.

Mei: What if we share other things that tell about our cultures? Have you ever seen the Dragon Dance at Chinese New Year? When my family and I saw it in San Francisco, I made a video of it.

Rick: Cool! I don't have video, but I could teach people how to do Irish dance. Some of my family play Irish instruments.

Carl: And stories! Our next-door neighbor, Mrs. Somé, is a *griot*. That's a person who tells or sings the historical stories of West Africa. She grew up with the *griot* tradition, and now she tells stories at our local library. I'm sure she would help us.

Jana: I want to add to Carl's suggestion. Along with stories and folk tales, we could also share our own experiences. For example, I could tell about how my mom and dad moved to Oak Valley from Bangalore. It was a big change! My sister and I were born here, and we're always pestering them to tell us what it was like to emigrate from India to America.

Mr. Lee: You all have great ideas! Are there any more suggestions you want to add?

(All of Mr. Lee's students raise their hands.)

Narrator: As you can see, the sunny day had turned into a storm—a *brainstorm*! Over the next few weeks, Mr. Lee asked the school principal and the other teachers about holding an International Day. Then he sent a letter home with students, inviting all the families to take part.

Chorus: What did they say?

Narrator: They said yes! Everyone was so excited. The teachers were excited, the parents were excited, and Mr. Lee's students—

Chorus: —were the most excited of all!

Narrator: That's right. Day after day, they came up with more ways to celebrate each other's cultures. They folded Japanese origami and wrote haiku. They made a mural about Ohlone people in early California. They found pictures of handmade crafts from Central America. They even recorded a speech about the contributions of each culture.

Chorus: That's amazing!

Narrator: Oh, that was just the beginning. Just listen to this—

Mr. Lee: So remember, many twentieth-century artists from California made a big impact on the cultural development of the United States. *(He sees that Jana has raised her hand.)* Yes, Jana?

Jana: That gives me another idea for our International Day. We could make a display to show that these artists represent many different cultures. I wonder if any of those artists have a connection to Oak Valley?

Carl: We could add the display to the gallery we made. It could be part of our "We Love Culture" exhibit. Did you know that the United States is one of the most culturally diverse countries in the world?

Mei: It's true! I found out some interesting facts as I was researching how to make a population map of the United States. People from all over the world already call America home, and immigrants continue to settle here.

Mr. Lee: I can see that you have all done your homework!

Miguel: That's good, because International Day is less than a week away!

Narrator: Finally, the big day came. That morning, Mr. Lee gave his class some final tips.

Mr. Lee: Be sure to greet everyone politely. Make eye contact and remember to smile. Listen carefully, in case someone has a question or does not understand something.

Mr. Lee's Class: Yes, Mr. Lee.

Mr. Lee: Oh, and one more thing. A surprise guest is joining us.

Chorus: A surprise guest? Who could it be?

Narrator: The students wondered, too. Then they opened the doors and invited all the families, neighbors, other students, and teachers to come inside. It was a great day.

Chorus: A great day!

Narrator: There was singing and dancing—

Chorus: Singing and dancing!

Narrator: Good food and games—

Chorus: Good food and games!

Narrator: Everybody learned a lot, and everybody had—

Chorus: —a wonderful time!

Narrator: And then—

Chorus: And then?

Narrator: Mr. Lee introduced a woman named Ms. Franklin. Now Ms. Franklin had been taking photographs all day. But who was she?

Chorus: A mom? A teacher? A neighbor?

Mr. Lee: I would like you all to meet Ms. Franklin. Ms. Franklin is the director of the Cultural Center. I wrote to her about the day we had to cancel our field trip. I told her about our plans.

Ms. Franklin: Hello! When Mr. Lee told me about how you planned an International Day of your own, I wanted to see it for myself. Now that I have, I am so impressed that I have a big announcement to make.

Chorus and Mr. Lee's class: What? What?

Narrator and Mr. Lee: Listen and find out!

Ms. Franklin: The Cultural Center plans to host a special exhibit inspired by— you! Our exhibit will show people how you planned an International Day right in your own community. It will show visitors from all over America how they can do this, too!

Everyone: Hurray!

Narrator: And that's the story of how one group of students turned a challenge into an opportunity. After all, sharing all our ideas is what makes America—

Everyone: A great place to live!

Write About It

If you could have an International Day with your class, what would you do? Describe the different kinds of food and activities your class could share.

Chapter 2

The Northeast

ESSENTIAL **EQ** QUESTION

Why Have People Moved To and From the Northeast?

In this chapter, you will explore how resources of the Northeast were used by early Native Americans. You will also discover how new ideas in this region formed the beginnings of our country. You will learn how the region's geography was favorable for powering the Industrial Revolution. You will also read about reform movements for women's rights, for the abolition of slavery, and for improvements in work conditions.

Talk About It COLLABORATE

Discuss the Northeast region with a partner. What do you know about people's reasons for coming to this region in the past? Why do you think people continue to move to the Northeast?

Inquiry Project

Write with a Point of View

In this project, you will use point of view to write a creative nonfiction story about changes that have happened in the Northeast since the Revolutionary War.

Project Checklist

☐ **Discuss** historical figures you've read about who lived in this region. Identify one that interests you the most.

☐ **Plan** your story. Decide on setting and conflict. The conflict should be an issue or problem from his or her time period. Outline the plot, including the resolution of the conflict.

☐ **Revise** your rough draft after rereading it and consulting a partner for feedback.

☐ **Present** your story to the class. Invite others to compare the points of view of your story and their stories.

☐ **Recall** facts, quotes, and other details about this figure. Consider his or her point of view. What might he or she have thought and felt about events during that time period?

My Research Plan

Write down any research questions you have that will help you plan your project. You can add questions as you carry out your research.

_____

_____

_____

Complete this chapter's Word Rater. Write notes as you learn more about each word.

abolitionist
☐ Know It!
☐ Heard It!
☐ Don't Know It!

My Notes

_____

_____

_____

charter
☐ Know It!
☐ Heard It!
☐ Don't Know It!

My Notes

_____

_____

_____

industrialization
☐ Know It!
☐ Heard It!
☐ Don't Know It!

My Notes

_____

_____

_____

negotiate
☐ Know It!
☐ Heard It!
☐ Don't Know It!

My Notes

_____

_____

_____

protest
☐ Know It!
☐ Heard It!
☐ Don't Know It!

My Notes

_____

_____

_____

quarry

My Notes

- ☐ Know It!
- ☐ Heard It!
- ☐ Don't Know It!

_____

_____

_____

raw material

My Notes

- ☐ Know It!
- ☐ Heard It!
- ☐ Don't Know It!

_____

_____

_____

revolutionary

My Notes

- ☐ Know It!
- ☐ Heard It!
- ☐ Don't Know It!

_____

_____

_____

suffrage

My Notes

- ☐ Know It!
- ☐ Heard It!
- ☐ Don't Know It!

_____

_____

_____

waterway

My Notes

- ☐ Know It!
- ☐ Heard It!
- ☐ Don't Know It!

_____

_____

_____

Lesson 1

How Did the Geography of the Northeast Influence the Way People Lived?

Lesson Outcomes

What Am I Learning?

In this lesson, you're going to use your investigative skills to explore the geographic features unique to the Northeast and how people use the resources of the Northeast to live.

Why Am I Learning It?

Reading and talking about the geography of the Northeast will help you learn more about the people who first lived there and what caused their communities to grow.

How Will I Know That I Learned It?

You will be able to explain the effect of the geographic features unique to the Northeast on the people who lived there.

Talk About It

COLLABORATE

Look closely at the picture. What geographic features do you see in this photo? What do you see that might have helped early peoples survive? What other resources might you need to live here?

Walden Pond in Massachusetts, inspired Henry David Thoreau

1 Inspect

Read Look at the title. Who do you think this text will be about?

Circle Find words you don't know to circle.

Underline Find and underline clues that help you answer:

- Who was Henry David Thoreau?
- When did he live?
- Where was the place he wrote about?

My Notes

_____

_____

_____

_____

_____

_____

_____

_____

A Writer at Walden Pond

Henry David Thoreau lived in the Northeast from 1817 until 1862. Growing up, Thoreau was inspired by the natural features of the Northeast. He enjoyed hiking in the mountains and forests. Author Ralph Waldo Emerson became Thoreau's mentor. Emerson encouraged Thoreau to write about what he loved — nature.

Thoreau is best known for the writing he did at Walden Pond in Massachusetts. He built a small cabin by the pond. He lived simply for more than two years, using only what he could grow or make himself from nearby resources. He explored the woods, rivers, and mountains of the Northeast. He wrote extensively about the plants and animals he encountered. The journal he kept was published in 1854 as *Walden, or Life in the Woods*.

This is a replica of Thoreau's cabin in the woods.

In Their Words... Henry David Thoreau

"I went to the woods because I wished to live deliberately, to front only the essential facts of life, and see if I could not learn what it had to teach, and not, when I came to die, discover that I had not lived."

—from *Walden, or Life in the Woods*, 1854

Henry David Thoreau

Thoreau was also a journalist, philosopher, and scientist. Many of his essays covered social issues. He was also skilled at surveying the local geography and making maps. He continued writing until his death in 1862. Many of his journals are still published and enjoyed today.

2 Find Evidence

Reread How did nature have an effect on Henry David Thoreau as a writer?

Underline Identify the natural features Thoreau studied and wrote about.

3 Make Connections

Talk What inspired Henry David Thoreau to move to Walden Pond? How did he plan to live? Why do you think the time Thoreau spent at Walden Pond was so important to him?

COLLABORATE

Explore Cause and Effect

An **effect** is what happened. A **cause** is why it happened.
To find the cause and effect:

1. **Read the text from beginning to end.**
   This gives you a complete overview of the material and helps you understand what the text is about.

2. **Reread the text and look for clues that tell you how people lived.**
   What did people do to adapt to the features around them? The result is the effect.

3. **Reread the text again and look for a detail that tells you why people adapted and lived that way.**
   What features led, or caused, people to adapt and live the way they did? This is the cause.

4. **Ask yourself: *What is the relationship between the cause and the effect?***
   Think about how a cause led to the effect.

 Based on the text you read, work with your class to complete the chart below.

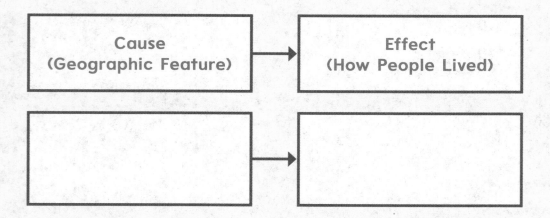

Cause (Geographic Feature)	Effect (How People Lived)

Investigate!

Read pages 64–73 in your Research Companion. Use your investigative skills to look for text evidence that tells you what features people encountered and how those features caused them to adapt. This chart will help you organize your notes.

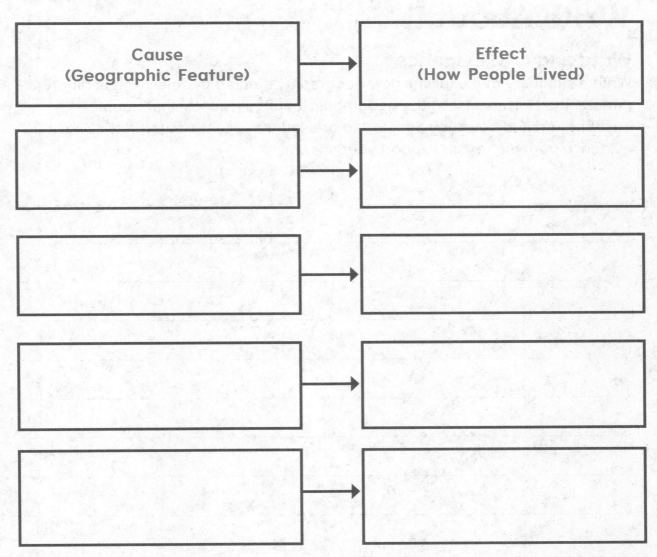

Cause (Geographic Feature)	Effect (How People Lived)

Think About It

Identify Effects

Review your research. Based on the information you have gathered, how do you think people used the geography of the Northeast when they first settled in the region?

Write About It

Write and Cite Evidence

Write a summary that explains how geography affected people living in different parts of the Northeast. List the geographic features (causes) that people encountered and how they adapted to or used those features (effects). Cite evidence from the text to support your answer.

_____

_____

_____

_____

_____

_____

_____

_____

_____

_____

Talk About It

Comprehend

With a partner, discuss why populations in the Northeast region grew and thrived using nearby geographic features and resources. Use evidence from the text to support your ideas.

ography

Connect to the

Pull It Together

Think about the lives of the Eastern Woodlands Native Americans and the first European settlers. How did the geography affect where they settled and how they lived? List three cause-and-effect relationships below.

1. _____

_____

_____

2. _____

_____

_____

3. _____

_____

_____

Inquiry Project Notes

_____

_____

_____

Lesson 2

Why Did Revolutionary Ideas Prosper in the Northeast?

Lesson Outcomes

What Am I Learning?

In this lesson, you're going to use your investigative skills to explore why new ideas prospered in the Northeast.

Why Am I Learning It?

Reading and talking about the history of the Northeast will help you learn how this area became known as "the cradle of liberty."

How Will I Know That I Learned It?

You will be able to explain how the revolution against Great Britain started in the Northeast.

Talk About It

COLLABORATE

Look at the image. Where do you think the people are going?

Pilgrims departing England

The Mayflower Compact

1 Inspect

Read Look at the title. What do you think the Mayflower Compact is?

Circle words you don't know.

Underline clues in the primary source that help you answer these questions:

- When was the Mayflower Compact written?
- When did they arrive in North America?
- Where is Plymouth?

My Notes

_____

_____

_____

_____

_____

_____

_____

_____

In the 1600s, people who lived in England had to worship in the Church of England. If they didn't they could be fined or imprisoned. The Pilgrims were a group of people who didn't agree with all of the teachings of the Church of England. They wanted to practice their own religion and live in their own community. However, they couldn't do this in England. In 1608, the Pilgrims went to live in Holland. Then in 1620, 100 people, including about 60 Pilgrims, set sail from England for North America on a ship called the *Mayflower*.

Before the Pilgrims landed in Massachusetts, leaders on the ship gathered to write the Mayflower Compact. Its purpose was to form a government and agree to follow any rules the group adopted. They did this for the good of the colony in hopes that working together would help the colony succeed.

The compact was signed by nearly all of the adult men on the ship. Although women were not part of creating the rules and did not sign the Compact, all members of the colony were required to follow the agreement. The Pilgrims elected a governor to run their government. This idea of self-government was an important idea for the formation of North American colonies.

Pilgrims on the Mayflower wrote down the rules of their new community in an agreement called the *Mayflower Compact*.

PRIMARY SOURCE

In Their Words...
The Mayflower Compact, 1620

(We) ". . . enact, constitute, and frame, such just and equal Laws, Ordinances, Acts, Constitutions and Offices . . . unto which we promise all due submission and obedience. In Witness whereof we have hereunto subscribed our names at Cape Cod the eleventh of November, in the Reign of our Sovereign Lord, King James of England, France and Ireland, the eighteenth, and of Scotland the fifty-fourth. Anno Domini, 1620."

2 Find Evidence

Reread What is the purpose of the Mayflower Compact?

Underline the words in the primary source that are about rules and government.

3 Make Connections

Talk Why are the ideas of the Mayflower Compact an important part of United States history?

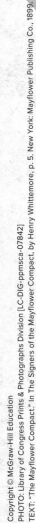

Explore Main Idea and Key Details

Each section of a text has a **main idea**. The main idea is the big idea of the text. The main idea is supported by **key details**. The key details tell more specific information. You can use the key details to help confirm the main idea.

To identify the main idea and key details:

1. **Read the section of text.**

2. **Think about what the section of text is mostly about.**

3. **Write down what you think the main idea is.**

4. **Reread the text.** Search for key details that support the main idea. Write the supporting details next to the main ideas.

5. **If you cannot find details that support your main idea, rethink the main idea.** Then, reread the text and look for key details that support that main idea.

COLLABORATE Based on the text you read, work with your class to complete the chart below.

Main Idea	Key Details
The Pilgrims came to North America to have more freedom.	

Investigate!

Read pages 74–83 in your Research Companion. Use your investigative skills to look for text evidence that tells you the main idea and key details of parts of the text.

The economies of the New England Colonies and Middle Colonies were different.	

Think About It

Review your research. Based on the information you have gathered, why do you think revolutionary ideas prospered in the Northeast?

Write About It

Define
What is a protest?

_____

_____

_____

Write and Cite Evidence
How can protests spark a change? Use facts from the texts to explain your response.

_____

_____

_____

_____

_____

_____

_____

_____

Talk About It

Explain

Share your response with a partner. Together discuss how protests led to revolutionary ideas in the Northeast.

 # Connect to the

Pull It Together

How did the events of the Revolutionary era make the Northeast a key location for people both in the past and today?

_____

_____

_____

_____

_____

_____

_____

Inquiry Project Notes

_____

_____

_____

_____

Lesson 3

What Conditions Powered the Industrial Revolution?

Lesson Outcomes

What Am I Learning?
In this lesson, you're going to use your investigative skills to explore inventions that helped bring about the Industrial Revolution.

Why Am I Learning It?
Reading and talking about how new technology, inventors, and businesses worked together during the Industrial Revolution will help you understand the foundations for the modern world.

How Will I Know That I Learned It?
You will be able to explain what conditions were in place that allowed the Industrial Revolution to happen.

Talk About It
COLLABORATE

Look closely at the picture. How many kinds of transportation can you find? What are the advantages of each?

Traveling on the Erie Canal

1 Inspect

Read Look at the title and then the image. What do they tell you about the subject matter you will read about?

Highlight Find the reasons the Erie Canal was needed.

Underline Find the benefits provided by the canal as it was being built and afterward.

My Notes

_____

_____

_____

_____

_____

_____

_____

_____

_____

The Erie Canal

Early Americans used rivers to travel and transport goods. However, the rivers did not always go where people needed them to go. People solved that problem by digging canals. These were channels that connected rivers and lakes.

The most famous was the Erie Canal in New York State. Because the land along the route was not flat, engineers included 83 locks. Locks raise or lower water so boats can travel from one level of water to another level of water.

Workers completed the Erie Canal in 1825. It created a waterway from the Great Lakes to the Atlantic Ocean. Mules or horses walked a path next to the canal to tow flat boats and barges down the canal. Later, steamboats traveled the canal. Passengers could travel 290 miles from Albany, New York, to Buffalo, New York, in just five days. Before the canal, such a trip took two weeks by wagon.

The canal brought settlers farther west. They sent produce and other goods back and forth to the eastern cities. Shipping prices decreased by 90 percent. The canal also made New York City the nation's most important seaport.

DeWitt Clinton marked the opening of the Erie Canal by pouring water from Lake Erie into the Atlantic Ocean.

Low Bridge, Everybody Down

Fifteen years on the Erie Canal
We've hauled some barges in our day
Filled with lumber, coal, and hay
And every inch of the way we know
From Albany to Buffalo

Chorus:

Low bridge, everybody down
Low bridge for we're coming to a town
And you'll always know your neighbor
And you'll always know your pal
If you've ever navigated on the Erie Canal

—*Thomas S. Allen, 1905*

Northeastern view of the locks at Lockport, New York

2 Find Evidence

Reread How did the Erie Canal influence the people and industries of the northeastern United States?

Circle the length of the trip between Albany and Buffalo.

3 Make Connections

Draw What did the boats that traveled the Erie Canal look like? How were they powered? On a separate sheet of paper, draw a picture of a scene that answers these questions.

Explore Main Idea and Key Details

The **main idea** is the most important idea the author presents in a section of text. **Key details** give important information to support the main idea.

To find the main idea and key details:

1. **Reread the text.**
   This will help you better understand what ideas are presented.

2. **Identify the key details.**
   Look for clues about details that support important ideas.

3. **Think about what the key details have in common to figure out the main idea of the section.**

COLLABORATE   Based on the text you read, work with your class to complete the chart below.

Main Idea	Key Details

Investigate!

Read pages 84–93 in your Research Companion. Use your investigative skills to look for details in the text that help you identify a main idea. This chart will help you organize your notes.

Main Idea	Key Details

Think About It

Review Your Research

Based on the information you have gathered, how do you think people reacted to the changes brought by the Industrial Revolution?

Write About It

Summarize

What conditions marked the launch of the Industrial Revolution?

_____

_____

_____

_____

_____

Write and Cite Evidence

How did the Industrial Revolution evolve as new inventions and developments became available? Use facts from the texts to explain your response.

_____

_____

_____

_____

_____

_____

_____

_____

Talk About It

Explain

Discuss with a partner how the lives of people changed over the course of the Industrial Revolution.

 History

Connect to the

Pull It Together

What conditions in the Industrial Revolution caused people to move to the Northeast over time?

_____

_____

_____

_____

_____

_____

Inquiry Project Notes

_____

_____

_____

_____

_____

Lesson 4

What Attracts People to the Northeast Today?

Lesson Outcomes

What Am I Learning?

In this lesson, you're going to use your investigative skills to explore how reform movements, job opportunities, and tourist attractions draw people to the Northeast.

Why Am I Learning It?

Reading and talking about the opportunities of the Northeast will help you learn why it is an important region.

How Will I Know That I Learned It?

You will be able to write a persuasive letter explaining what attracts people to the Northeast region.

Talk About It

COLLABORATE

Look closely at the picture. What do you notice about the people in this statue? Why do you think this statue was made?

This statue depicts an important moment in women's fight for the right to vote.

Read Look at the title and first sentence. What do you think this text will be about?

Circle words you don't know.

Underline clues that help you answer these questions:

- Who attended the Seneca Falls Convention?
- What happened at the Seneca Falls Convention?

My Notes

_____

_____

_____

_____

_____

_____

_____

_____

The Seneca Falls Convention

On July 19, 1848, a women's rights convention was held in Seneca Falls, New York. This was the first time such an event occurred in the United States. The purpose was to discuss the social, civil, and religious rights of women. This meeting was organized by Lucretia Mott and Elizabeth Cady Stanton, two leaders in the women's rights movement.

At the meeting, Stanton read a document called the Declaration of Sentiments and Grievances. A grievance is an official statement of a complaint about something believed to be wrong or unfair. She based this document on the Declaration of Independence. The Declaration of Sentiments and Grievances outlined the wrongs done to women in the United States. It called on women to organize and petition for their rights. All attendees voted in favor of the declaration.

This sign marks the location of the Seneca Falls Convention.

TEXT: (t) The Declaration of Independence, Preamble, July 4, 1776. The National Archives and Records Administration. (b) Mott, Lucretia, Mary Ann McClintock, Elizabeth Cady Stanton, Jane C. Hunt and Martha C. Wright, Declaration of Sentiments and Resolutions. Woman's Rights Convention, Seneca Falls, New York, July 19-20, 1848. Library of Congress, Rare Book and Special Collections Division, National American Woman Suffrage Association Collection.

In Their Words...
Thomas Jefferson

We hold these truths to be self-evident, that all men are created equal, that they are endowed by their Creator with certain unalienable rights, that among these are life, liberty, and the pursuit of Happiness.

—from the Declaration of Independence, 1776

In Their Words...
Elizabeth Cady Stanton

We hold these truths to be self-evident: that all men and women are created equal; that they are endowed by their Creator with certain inalienable rights, that among these are life, liberty, and the pursuit of happiness.

—from the Declaration of Sentiments and Grievances, 1848

The convention then discussed specific rights that women should have, including the right to vote. At that time, only men could vote, not women.

From 1848 on, a women's rights convention was held every year. Because of the meeting in Seneca Falls and the hard work in the years that followed, the 19th Amendment was passed in 1920, giving women the right to vote. However, women of color did not fully benefit from this amendment.

2 Find Evidence

Reread How are the Declaration of Independence and the Declaration of Sentiments and Grievances alike? How are they different?

What two words did Elizabeth Cady Stanton add? How do those words change the meaning of the Declaration of Independence?

3 Make Connections

Talk Discuss with a partner why the Declaration of Sentiments and Grievances was so important for women's rights in the United States. What details in the text support your answer?

COLLABORATE

Explore Main Idea and Key Details

The **main idea** is the most important idea the author presents in a section of text. **Key details** give important information to support the main idea.

To identify the main idea and key details:

1. **Reread the text.**
   This will help you better understand what ideas are presented.

2. **Identify the key details.**
   Look for clues and important details in the text.

3. **Think about what the key details have in common to figure out the main idea of the section.**

Based on the text you read, work with your class to complete the chart below.

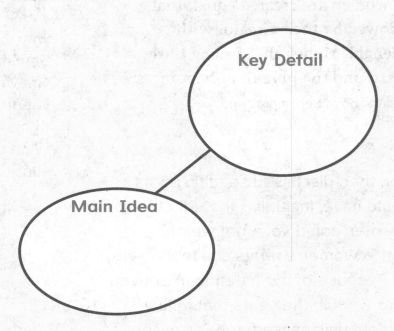

Key Detail

Main Idea

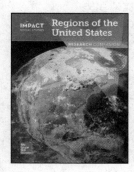

Investigate!

Read pages 94–103 in your Research Companion. Use your investigative skills to identify the main idea and details about what attracts people to the Northeast.

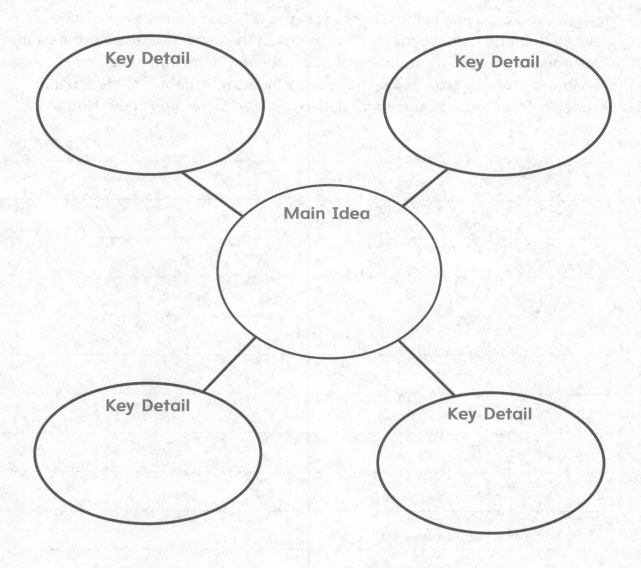

Key Detail

Key Detail

Main Idea

Key Detail

Key Detail

Think About It

Review Your Research

Based on the information you have gathered, think about the different reasons people have been drawn to the Northeast.

Write About It

Take a Stand

Imagine you are living in the Northeast in the 1800s and want to persuade a relative or friend to move there. Choose one of the aspects of the Northeast that you read about, such as educational advancement, immigration, reform movements, or city growth. Write a letter using specfic details related to that aspect in order to persuade your relative or friend to join you in the Northeast.

_____

_____

_____

_____

_____

_____

_____

_____

_____

_____

Talk About It

Explain

Read your letter to a partner. Have your partner decide if the letter is persuasive enough to convince someone to move to the Northeast.

History

Connect to the

Pull It Together

From what you read in this lesson, think about the reasons people come to the Northeast. Choose one to write about. Write about how the benefits of living in the Northeast have changed over time.

_____

_____

_____

_____

Inquiry Project Notes

_____

_____

_____

_____

Lesson 5

What Links the Northeast to the World?

Lesson Outcomes

What Am I Learning?

In this lesson, you're going to use your investigative skills to explore important ways that the Northeast is connected to the world.

Why Am I Learning It?

Reading and talking about how the Northeast is linked to the world will help you understand the importance of this region.

How Will I Know That I Learned It?

You will be able to give examples of people, places, and organizations from the Northeast that have had an important effect on the world.

Talk About It

COLLABORATE

Examine the flags in the picture. What does each flag represent? Why do you think they are all together?

The United Nations Building

Copyright © McGraw-Hill Education   © Digital Archive Japan/Alamy

Many Nations Meet in One City

1 Inspect

Read the text. What connection does the United Nations have to the Northeast? What connection does it have to the world?

Circle words you don't know.

Underline clues that help you answer these questions:

- **What** is the United Nations? What does it do?
- **Where** is its headquarters, or main office?
- **How** has it affected the world?

My Notes

_____

_____

_____

_____

_____

_____

One of the most important buildings in the world is in the Northeast. It is the United Nations headquarters, a meeting place for people from many countries. It is located in New York City.

After World War II, people in many different countries wanted to find a way to prevent future wars. They saw the terrible harm that war had caused, including the loss of lives, the destruction of property, and the spread of poverty and hunger.

On June 26, 1945, representatives from 50 countries signed the United Nations **Charter**. This important agreement established the United Nations, an organization created to encourage countries to work together for peace.

The flag of the United Nations

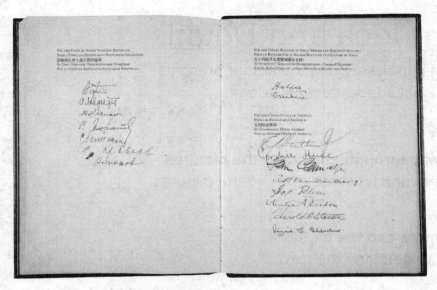

The charter of the United Nations

PRIMARY SOURCE

In Their Words...
United Nations Charter

We the peoples of the United Nations determined

- to save succeeding generations from the scourge of war, which twice in our lifetime has brought untold sorrow to mankind, and

- to reaffirm faith in fundamental human rights, in the dignity and worth of the human person, in the equal rights of men and women and of nations large and small . . .

—*United Nations Charter, 1945*

2 Find Evidence

Reread What details help you understand why many countries decided to form the United Nations?

Underline the problems that the signers of the United Nations Charter hoped to solve.

3 Make Connections

Talk Why is New York City a good location for the United Nations?

Connect to Now Why is the United Nations still important today?

Explore Main Idea and Details

The **main idea** is the most important point the author presents. **Details** are the key points that support the main idea.

To find the main idea:

1. **Read the text all the way through and study the pictures.** This will help you understand what the text and the pictures are about.

2. **Look again at the pictures and the captions.** How do they help you understand the text?

3. **Reread the text.** Ask yourself, "What sentences help identify the main idea of the text? How can those sentences be restated as one main idea? What details support this idea?"

 Based on the pictures and the text you read, work with your class to complete the chart below.

Main Idea	Details

Investigate!

Read pages 104–111 in your Research Companion. Use your investigative skills to look for key details that tell you the main ideas of the text. This chart will help you organize your main ideas. Copy the chart below to add a section for each passage.

Main Idea	Details

Main Idea	Details

Main Idea	Details

Main Idea	Details

Think About It

Review Your Research

Based on the information you have gathered, think about the importance of the Northeast region of the United States and what links it to the rest of the world.

Write About It

Write and Cite Evidence

In your opinion, how has the Northeast region been important to the world? List three ideas to share with others. Use facts from the texts to support your opinion.

_____

_____

_____

_____

_____

_____

_____

_____

_____

_____

_____

Talk About It

Explain

Talk with a small group of classmates. Together discuss how the Northeast region and its people have impacted the world.

 eography

Connect to the

Pull It Together

How have the connections the Northeast has to the world influenced why people have moved there?

_____

_____

_____

_____

_____

_____

Inquiry Project Notes

_____

_____

_____

_____

_____

Why Have People Moved To and From the Northeast?

Inquiry Project

Write with a Point of View

Complete your story about how the Northeast changed since the Revolutionary War.

Complete Your Project

Use the checklist to evaluate your project. If you left anything out, here's your chance to fix it!

☐ Review facts about the person you chose as well as the setting and conflict. Make sure the person's point of view is clearly stated.

☐ Check that the conflict of the story is resolved by the end.

☐ Record any sources that you used for research.

☐ Reread your story. Check that it makes sense for the time period.

Share Your Project

☐ Practice reading your essay aloud before your presentation.

☐ Speak clearly so your audience can hear and understand you.

☐ Explain to your classmates why you chose your particular person.

☐ Listen carefully and answer any questions from your classmates.

Reflect on Your Project

Think about the work you did in this chapter and on your project. Use the questions below to help guide your thoughts.

1. Why did you select the topic that you wrote about in your story?

_____

2. How did you conduct your research? How did you make sure that your sources were reliable? _____

_____

3. Is there anything you would do differently next time?_____

_____

Chapter Connections

Use pictures, words, or both to reflect on what you learned in this chapter.

The most interesting thing I learned:

Something I learned from a classmate:

A connection I can make with my own life:

Chapter 3

The Southeast

How Has the Southeast Changed Over Time?

In this chapter, you'll read about change in the Southeast from life in early settlements to the economy today. You will read about how the growth of the region affected people's lives. You will also read about the rebuilding of the region after the Civil War and the growth of modern industries. All these factors will help you answer the Essential Question.

Talk About It COLLABORATE

Discuss with your partner questions you have about the Southeast region. As you research, think about what happened to native peoples and enslaved Africans. As you research, look for answers to your questions.

Inquiry Project

Southeast Region Newspaper Article

You will work with a team to create a newspaper article that explains a change in the Southeast over time. Write an article that reflects a change in government, geography, population, economics, or a topic of your own choice.

Project Checklist

- [ ] **List** topics that interest you about the Southeast.
- [ ] **Choose** and **Research** a topic that interests you most. Think about how your topic changed over time.
- [ ] **Describe** the important who, what, why, when, where, and how details about the topic.
- [ ] **Write** a newspaper article to describe the change related to your topic.
- [ ] **Choose** a headline to describe and make people want to read your article.

My Research Plan

Write down any research questions you have that will help you plan your project. You can add questions as you carry out your research.

_____

_____

_____

_____

Explore / Words

Complete this chapter's Word Rater.
Write notes as you learn more about each word.

boycott

☐ Know It!
☐ Heard It!
☐ Don't Know It!

My Notes

_____
_____
_____

commerce

☐ Know It!
☐ Heard It!
☐ Don't Know It!

My Notes

_____
_____
_____

estuary

☐ Know It!
☐ Heard It!
☐ Don't Know It!

My Notes

_____
_____
_____

evacuate

☐ Know It!
☐ Heard It!
☐ Don't Know It!

My Notes

_____
_____
_____

plantation

☐ Know It!
☐ Heard It!
☐ Don't Know It!

My Notes

_____
_____
_____

proximity

My Notes

☐ Know It!

_____

☐ Heard It!

_____

☐ Don't Know It!

_____

rural

My Notes

☐ Know It!

_____

☐ Heard It!

_____

☐ Don't Know It!

_____

secede

My Notes

☐ Know It!

_____

☐ Heard It!

_____

☐ Don't Know It!

_____

sharecropper

My Notes

☐ Know It!

_____

☐ Heard It!

_____

☐ Don't Know It!

_____

yeoman

My Notes

☐ Know It!

_____

☐ Heard It!

_____

☐ Don't Know It!

_____

How Do People and the Environment Interact?

Lesson Outcomes

What Am I Learning?

In this lesson, you're going to use your investigative skills to explore the physical features unique to the Southeast and see how the people and the environment are connected.

Why Am I Learning It?

Reading and talking about the physical features of the Southeast will help you learn more about the connection between people and their environment.

How Will I Know That I Learned It?

You will be able to explain the effect of the environment of the Southeast on the people who lived there, and how the people use and change the environment.

Talk About It

COLLABORATE

Look closely at the picture. How might early Southeast peoples have adapted to living in this environment? How might early people have used the natural resources here? How might people today adapt to this environment and use these resources?

Grassy marshes can be found in the Southeast region.

Cherokee Basket Weaving

1 Inspect

Look at the photo. What does it show? What do you think this article will be about? Now read the article.

Circle words you don't know.

Underline clues that answer these questions:

- How were the baskets made?
- What materials were used?
- Who made them?
- How were the baskets used?

My Notes

_____

_____

_____

_____

_____

_____

_____

_____

_____

_____

The Native American people, the Cherokee, originally lived in the Southeast. The Cherokee people have been making baskets for thousands of years. Cherokee baskets are known for their complex designs and contrasting colors. They are made from natural materials.

Cherokee women use fibers from cane, oak, hickory, and honeysuckle plants and trees that are readily available in the environment. They use sharp tools to strip the bark and leaves from the plants. Then, they cut the material into long, thin strips. These strips are woven together to make strong baskets.

Basket weavers use natural plant dyes to color the strips. The most common dyes are bloodroot for a yellow color, black walnut for brown, and elderberries for red.

The pattern, or arrangement, of the woven strips gives Cherokee baskets their unique designs. Patterns are not written down but are shared among family members. These patterns are often inspired by nature. The creative designs represent features of the environment, such as mountains or rivers.

Cherokee Basket

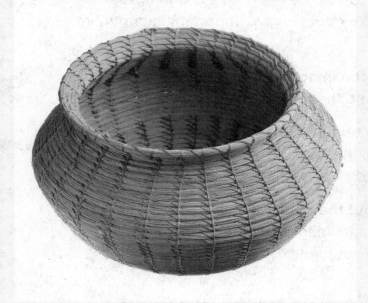

Cherokee people wove baskets by hand from natural materials.

In the past, baskets were used in everyday life. They were used to store food in the home. Some baskets had straps added so men could carry hunting tools with them. Other baskets were woven to be used as strainers for catching and holding fish. If cared for, a basket could last for several generations. Today, Cherokee baskets are still functional, but they are also considered works of art.

2 Find Evidence

Look Again What natural resources can you observe were used in a Cherokee basket?

Underline the ways basket weavers were influenced by nature when they were making baskets.

3 Make Connections

Talk In a small group, discuss how Cherokee baskets were made. What parts of the natural environment were used? How did nature inspire the weavers? Use details from the text as examples.

COLLABORATE

Explore Main Idea and Key Details

Identifying key details in the text and visuals will help you better understand big ideas about a topic. The **main idea** is the most important idea about a topic. **Key details** give important information that supports the main idea.

1. **Read the text and look at the images.**
   This will help you understand the topic.

2. **Look for key details in the text and images.**
   Identify important details in the text and images. What do these details describe or explain?

3. **Use key details to figure out the main idea.**
   Use key details in the text and images to identify the main idea, or most important point, about the text.

Based on the text you read, work with your class to complete the chart below.

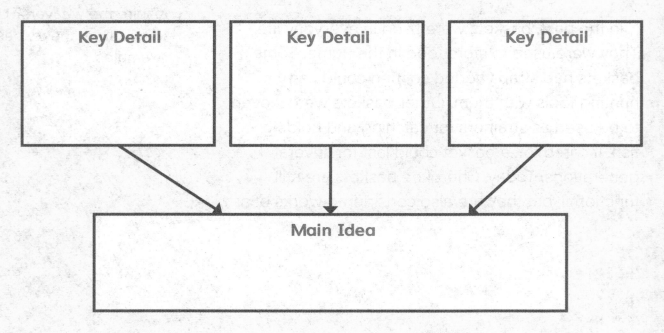

Key Detail	Key Detail	Key Detail

Main Idea

Investigate!

Read pages 124–133 in your Research Companion. Use your investigative skills to look for details that describe the environment of the Southeast and how the people interacted with it. This chart will help you organize your notes.

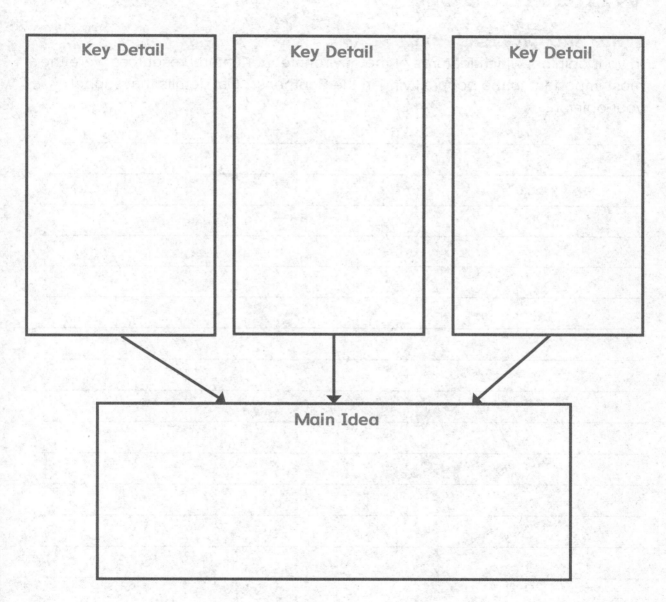

Key Detail	Key Detail	Key Detail

Main Idea

Think About It

Review Your Research

Review your research. Based on the information you have gathered, how do you think people and the environment interact in the Southeast?

Write About It

Write and Cite Evidence

In your opinion, which features of the environment or natural resources were the most important to the people living in the Southeast? List details that support your opinion.

_____

_____

_____

_____

_____

_____

_____

_____

_____

_____

_____

_____

_____

_____

Talk About It

Paraphrase

With a partner, take turns reading your opinions and supporting details. Paraphrase your partner's opinion and discuss why you agree or disagree with his or her opinion.

graphy

Connect to the

Pull It Together

Think about the environmental features of the Southeast that you read about in this lesson. How did geography affect the way people interacted with the environment of the Southeast? How did this change the region over time?

_____

_____

_____

_____

_____

_____

_____

Inquiry Project Notes

_____

_____

_____

_____

_____

_____

Lesson 2

What Made the Southeast Grow During the 1700s?

Lesson Outcomes

What Am I Learning?

In this lesson, you're going to use your investigative skills to identify causes for the growth of the Southeast region in the 1700s.

Why Am I Learning It?

Reading and talking about these causes will help you understand how and why the Southeast grew during the 1700s.

How Will I Know That I Learned It?

You will be able to identify the most important causes of the growth of the Southeast and how growth affected the people of the region.

Talk About It

COLLABORATE

Look closely at the picture. What do you think might happen at this building? Does this building remind you of any other buildings?

Revolutionary Ideas

1 Inspect

Read Look at the title. What does the word *revolutionary* mean to you?

- **Circle** words and phrases you don't know.
- **Underline** clues that help you answer the questions Who, What, When, Where, or Why.
- **Highlight** important words that tell you what caused something to happen.

My Notes

_____

_____

_____

_____

_____

_____

_____

_____

_____

_____

_____

During the 1770s, Virginia was one of the colonies ruled by the British government. British laws required colonists to pay steep taxes. Many Americans felt these laws were unfair. Many colonists thought they should be able to govern themselves. Protests had already begun in the Northeast.

In March 1775, representatives met in Richmond, Virginia, to discuss what to do. These men, including George Washington and Thomas Jefferson, were elected to represent the main settlements of Virginia. Many of the representatives talked about waiting to ask the British to reduce taxes.

After days of debate, a man named Patrick Henry spoke to the representatives. Henry's passionate speech described the British acts of war already happening in the Northeast. He rallied the men to see themselves as Americans, not just as Virginians. Henry's famous line, "give me liberty or give me death," was an important moment. The representatives voted to organize soldiers to fight the British. George Washington was later chosen to lead the Continental Army, which won the Revolutionary War.

Patrick Henry delivered his "Give me liberty or give me death!" speech in Richmond, Virginia, on March 23, 1775.

PRIMARY SOURCE

In Their Words... Patrick Henry

"Our brethren are already in the field! Why stand we here idle? What is it that gentlemen wish? What would they have? Is life so dear, or peace so sweet, as to be purchased at the price of chains and slavery? Forbid it, Almighty God! I know not what course others may take; but as for me, give me liberty or give me death!"

—from a speech given to the Virginia Convention in Richmond, Virginia, March 23, 1775

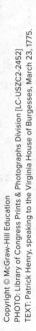

2 Find Evidence

Reread What did many of the Virginia representatives want to do about the conflict with the British? What was the purpose of Patrick Henry's speech? What words did he use to let you know his purpose?

Underline the events or dates leading up to the Revolutionary War. In your opinion, what role did Patrick Henry play in the American Revolution?

3 Make Connections

Talk Discuss with a partner the reasons Patrick Henry gave for needing to fight against the British. What effect did Patrick Henry's speech have on the listeners?

Explore Cause and Effect

A **cause** is why something happens. An **effect** is the result of what happens. An event can be either a cause or an effect.

1. **Read the text all the way through.**
   This will help you understand what the text is about.

2. **Look for words and phrases that signal cause-and-effect relationships.**
   Such signal words and phrases include *cause, effect, because, so,* and *due to.*

3. **Identify events that are linked to signal words.**
   Look for clues in the text that indicate which events caused a change and which events were the effect.

4. **Be aware that a cause can have more than one effect, and an effect can have more than one cause.**
   As you read about each event, notice cases in which more than one cause or effect is indicated.

Based on the text you read, work with your class to complete the chart below.

Cause		Effect
	$\longrightarrow$	

Investigate!

Read pages 134–143 in your Research Companion. Use your investigative skills to identify the cause-and-effect relationships that show what caused the Southeast to grow in the 1700s. This chart will help you organize your notes.

Cause	Effect
→	
→	
→	
→	
→	

Think About It

Identify Causes

Review your research. Based on the information you have gathered, what causes had the biggest effect on making the Southeast grow in this time period?

Write About It

Describe a Key Cause and Effect

Choose one of the causes that you think most influenced the growth of the Southeast. Write a paragraph describing how this cause affected the Southeast in the 1700s.

_____

_____

_____

_____

_____

_____

_____

_____

_____

_____

_____

Talk About It

Support Your Viewpoint

With a partner, share your ideas about different causes and effects for Southeast growth. Discuss why they weren't as important as the main cause you identified.

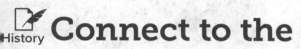 # Connect to the

Pull It Together

Think about the growth of the Southeast in the 1700s. How did the events and decisions of the time change the Southeast?

_____

_____

_____

_____

_____

_____

Inquiry Project Notes

_____

_____

_____

_____

_____

What Conflicts Changed the Southeast?

Lesson Outcomes

What Am I Learning?

In this lesson, you're going to use your investigative skills to explore how conflicts about Native Americans, slavery, and civil rights for African Americans shaped the Southeast.

Why Am I Learning It?

Reading and talking about the conflicts will help you learn about what has shaped the Southeast region of the United States.

How Will I Know That I Learned It?

You will be able to explain how the conflicts were resolved and how the Southeast region was affected as a result.

Talk About It
COLLABORATE

Look closely at the picture. What do you think is happening in the picture? What is the relationship between the people on shore and on the boat? How do you know?

Enslaved people received help escaping from the South.

1 Inspect

Read Look at the text and the image. What do you think the page will be about?

- **Circle** words and phrases that you do not know.
- **Underline** details that help you answer the questions *Who, What, Where, When,* or *Why.*
- **Discuss** with a partner some dangers enslaved people faced while traveling on the Underground Railroad.

My Notes

_____

_____

_____

_____

_____

_____

_____

_____

_____

_____

Harriet Tubman was born an enslaved person in Maryland. She worked in the fields and suffered terrible beatings. In 1849, she escaped slavery. She left her husband and family behind in order to escape. Even though she was in danger of being recaptured, she returned to the South at least 19 times to help others escape. She was determined to lead other enslaved people to freedom along the Underground Railroad. As a result, Harriet Tubman became famous as a leader, or conductor, on the Underground Railroad.

As a conductor, Tubman's job was to help enslaved people avoid capture. Sometimes, Tubman used the song "Wade in the Water" to tell those escaping slavery to get off a marked trail and into the water. She wanted to make sure the dogs used by those looking for them couldn't sniff out their trail. People walking through water did not leave a scent trail that dogs could follow. Because many enslaved people knew the secret meanings of these kinds of songs, they could be used to give directions. Read the words of "Wade in the Water."

In Their Words... African American Spiritual, "Wade in the Water"

Wade in the water,
Wade in the water, children,
Wade in the water,
God's gonna trouble the water.

See that host all dressed in white,
God's gonna trouble the water.
The leader looks like the Israelite,
God's gonna trouble the water. [Refrain]

See that band all dressed in red,
God's gonna trouble the water.
Looks like the band that Moses led,
God's gonna trouble the water. [Refrain]

2 Find Evidence

Reread What does the text suggest about the difficulties of traveling on the Underground Railroad? What details support your answer?

3 Make Connections

Talk Do you think people today still use the Big Dipper and North Star to find their way?

COLLABORATE

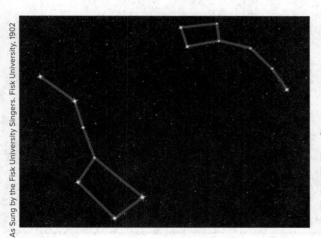

The Big Dipper points to the North Star, which is located at the handle of the Little Dipper.

When those escaping slavery traveled north, they traveled at night. They used the stars to help guide their journey. The North Star directed them. To locate the North Star, they looked to the night sky to find the Big Dipper and Little Dipper constellations. Travelers along the Underground Railroad were told to "Follow the Drinking Gourd," or the Big Dipper, which points to the North Star.

Explore Cause and Effect

A **cause** is why something happens. An **effect** is the result of what happens. An event can be either a cause or an effect.

To find a cause and its effect:

1. **Read the text all the way through.**
   This will help you understand what the text is about.

2. **Reread the text and look for a detail that tells you what or why something happened.**
   This is a cause. Circle it.

3. **Reread the text again and look for a detail that tells you the result of what happened.**
   This is the effect. Underline it.

4. **Finish the cause-and-effect statement.**
   _____ *happened because of* _____.

 Based on the text you read, work with your class to complete the chart below.

Cause	Effect
Harriet Tubman escaped slavery.	
Harriet Tubman sang "Wade in the Water."	

Investigate!

Read pages 144–153 in your Research Companion. Use your investigative skills to identify the causes and effects of conflicts between different groups in the Southeast region.

Cause	Effect

Think About It

Review your research. Based on the information you have gathered, how did individuals and groups respond to conflicts in the Southeast?

Write About It

Write and Cite Evidence

How did reading about the Indian Removal Act help you better understand the Native American experience in the nineteenth century? Consider what the text says about the journey and what it must have been like to leave their homes.

_____

_____

_____

_____

_____

_____

_____

_____

_____

_____

_____

_____

_____

_____

Talk About It

Compare and Contrast

Exchange journals with a classmate. Compare and contrast events and feelings. Discuss ways the removal of Native Americans could have been avoided.

 ## Connect to the

Pull It Together

From what you read in this lesson, think about how different people responded to conflicts in the Southeast. How did these conflicts affect the way of life of different groups of people of the Southeast? How did individuals and groups resist unfair treatment?

_____

_____

_____

_____

_____

_____

Inquiry Project Notes

_____

_____

_____

_____

_____

_____

Lesson 4

How Has the Southeast Reinvented Itself?

Lesson Outcomes

What Am I Learning?

In this lesson, you are going to use your investigative skills to explore how the Southeast reinvented itself after the Civil War.

Why Am I Learning It?

Reading and talking about the changes that took place in the Southeast will help you understand how it became the important region it is today.

How Will I Know That I Learned It?

You will be able to explain the conditions that changed the Southeast and how it continues to develop today.

Talk About It

Look closely at the picture. What are some ways dams could benefit a region?

The Norris Dam in eastern Tennessee was built as part of the Tennessee Valley Authority project in the 1930s.

Copyright © McGraw-Hill Education
tankbmb/Getty Images

1 Inspect

Read Read the heading. What do you think this heading refers to?

Highlight how the project changed through time.

Circle the benefits provided by the creation of the Tennessee Valley Authority.

My Notes

_____

_____

_____

_____

_____

_____

_____

_____

_____

_____

_____

Tennessee Valley Authority

The Tennessee River Valley covers parts of the Southeast. In the past, during dry seasons, the river became little more than a trickle. In other seasons, heavy rainfall caused it to flood low-lying areas. Few industries existed in the area, so many people who lived there did not have jobs. During the 1930s, the region suffered even more job loss because of the Great Depression.

President Franklin D. Roosevelt created a number of programs to help citizens during the Great Depression, including the Tennessee Valley Authority (TVA). The TVA supplied jobs for many workers, and it also controlled flooding and provided the area with electricity.

Construction of dams in the TVA program provided jobs for people in the Tennessee River Valley region.

This promotional poster created during the 1940s highlights the early progress made by the TVA.

Not everyone was pleased with the TVA program. Local utility companies tried to stop the TVA's progress by filing lawsuits, but they failed. In order to complete the huge project, the government had to move entire towns. For the people living in these towns, the move created great hardship.

Despite the controversy, the TVA had many successes. Local people received jobs. Dams controlled the flow of the water and generated electricity. TVA experts taught people better farming methods and replanted trees. Erosion no longer destroyed fertile soil. The rivers in the Tennessee Valley became easier to travel. The water quality increased, and people could boat and swim in the waterways as well.

Today, the TVA employs more than 10,000 people. Water quality is protected, and the TVA takes care of 293,000 acres of land, including more than 80 sites for public recreation. The TVA has made great strides toward protecting the environment by reducing smoke and other emissions from the power plants. In addition to jobs at the TVA itself, the surrounding region claims more than 60,000 jobs at companies that support the TVA.

2 Find Evidence

Reread What effect did the TVA have on the people who lived in the Tennessee River Valley?

Underline the numbers significant to the TVA's operation.

3 Make Connections

Write What difficulties did the creators of the TVA face?

COLLABORATE

Explore Main Idea and Key Details

The **main idea** is the most important point the author presents in a section of text. **Key details** give important information to support the main idea.

To find the main idea and key details:

1. **Reread the text.**
   This will help you better understand what ideas are presented.

2. **Identify the key details.**
   Look for clues about details that support important ideas.

3. **Think about what the key details have in common to figure out the main idea of the section.**

 Based on the text you read, work with your class to complete the chart below.

Main Idea	Key Details

Investigate!

Read pages 154–163 in your Research Companion. Use your investigative skills to look for text evidence that offers details that support a main idea. This chart will help you organize your notes.

Main Idea	Key Details

Think About It

Review
Review your research. Based on the information you have gathered, how did the Southeast reinvent itself?

Write About It

Define
What does the term *sharecropper* mean? Was it a fair system?

_____

_____

_____

_____

_____

_____

_____

Write and Cite Evidence
In what ways did the Southeast make use of its natural and human resources to prosper? Use facts from the texts to explain your response.

_____

_____

_____

_____

_____

Talk About It

Explain

Share your response in a small group discussion. Together talk about how the Southeast reinvented itself after the Civil War.

 **Connect to the**

Pull It Together

Think about how the Southeast developed after the Civil War. In what ways did this period help show how the Southeast changed over time?

_____

_____

_____

_____

_____

_____

_____

Inquiry Project Notes

_____

_____

_____

_____

_____

How Do Citizens of the Southeast Help Each Other and the World?

Lesson Outcomes

What Am I Learning?

In this lesson, you are going to use your investigative skills to explore how citizens from the Southeast take action to help each other and the world.

Why Am I Learning It?

Reading and talking about the positive actions of citizens in the Southeast will help you understand how the needs of others are met.

How Will I Know That I Learned It?

You will be able to explain how citizens in the Southeast overcome challenges and disasters.

Talk About It
COLLABORATE

Look closely at the picture. How would you describe what is happening? What can you tell about the destruction caused by a hurricane?

Volunteers help clear debris from homes after Hurricane Katrina hit New Orleans, Louisiana.

Building for Good

Copyright © McGraw-Hill Education

1 Inspect

Review Look at the title and read the lesson question. What do you already know about Habitat for Humanity?

Underline the reasons Habitat for Humanity works to help others.

Highlight the accomplishments made by Habitat for Humanity over the years.

My Notes

_____

_____

_____

_____

_____

_____

_____

_____

_____

Habitat for Humanity International opened in 1976 in Atlanta, Georgia. Founders Millard and Linda Fuller wanted to help people afford a decent place to live. With the help of volunteers, the Fullers built homes for needy people at no profit. The new homeowners made house payments to a fund. The fund was used to build more homes for other needy people. The idea caught on.

In 1984, former U.S. President Jimmy Carter and his wife Rosalynn became Habitat volunteers. Photographs of Carter building houses brought attention to the charity. In Carter's first project in New York City, he helped 19 families receive safe, decent housing. That experience inspired Carter to start a yearly event called Carter's Work Project. Each year, the event is held in a different city.

Habitat's work has continued to expand. Habitat opened ReStore, a retail shop that sells new and used furniture, appliances, and building materials at low prices. Not only does the program keep these items out of landfills, but the money it earns supports Habitat's charity work. Habitat also started a relief program. The program helps those whose homes have been destroyed in hurricanes and other disasters.

Habitat programs now exist in about 1,400 communities across the United States and in about 70 other countries around the world. Volunteers of all ages help Habitat fulfill their mission. Through Habitat, 13 million people have gained safe and affordable places to live.

Former President Jimmy Carter and his wife, Rosalynn, support Habitat for Humanity through participating in projects.

PRIMARY SOURCE

In Their Words... Jimmy Carter

To have a decent place to live is a basic human right. And also to have a chance to live in peace and to have adequate health care and adequate education, so you can take advantage of your talents.

—Former President Jimmy Carter, 2017

2 Find Evidence

Determine How did Jimmy Carter make a difference in Habitat for Humanity's programs?

Underline the role of individuals in Habitat's work.

3 Make Connections

Talk Discuss with a partner how Habitat homeowners and workers help provide housing for others.

COLLABORATE

Explore Important Details

Details provide more information about the main idea of a text. **Important details** help readers to understand the topic. Important details can include examples, descriptions, or explanations.

To understand important details:

1. **Read the text once all the way through.**

2. **Reread the text and look for specific names, numbers, and actions.**

3. **Think about what the information helps you to understand.**

 Based on the text you read, work with your class to complete the chart below.

Important Detail from Text	What It Explains	What It Helps Me Understand
With the help of volunteers, the Fullers built homes for needy people at no profit. The new homeowners made house payments to a fund. The fund was used to build more homes for other needy people.		

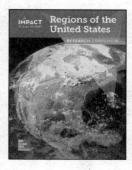

Investigate!

Read pages 164–171 in your Research Companion. Use your investigative skills to look for text evidence that tells you what happened and why the event is important. This chart will help you organize your notes.

Important Detail from Text	What It Explains	What It Helps Me Understand

Think About It

Review

Based on the information you have gathered, in what ways do citizens of the Southeast help each other and the world?

Write About It

Contrast

What are the benefits and drawbacks of living near the ocean?

_____

_____

_____

_____

Write and Cite Evidence

In what ways did Hurricane Katrina affect the Southeast? What changes came about because of it? How did people of the Southeast come together because of Katrina? Use facts from the texts to explain your response.

_____

_____

_____

_____

_____

_____

Talk About It

Explain

With a partner, talk about how people of the Southeast helped each other and pets after Hurricane Katrina. Discuss other ways people of the Southeast help others.

Connect to the

Pull it Together

Think about all the ways people of the Southeast help each other and the world. How does this help show the impact of people of the Southeast region of today?

_____

_____

_____

_____

_____

_____

_____

Inquiry Project Notes

_____

_____

_____

_____

How Has the Southeast Changed Over Time?

Inquiry Project

Southeast Region Newspaper Article

Remember, for this project you will create a newspaper article that shows a change in the Southeast. Your story should focus on a change in government, geography, population, economics, or a topic of your own choice.

Complete Your Project

Use the checklist to evaluate your project. If you left anything out, here's your chance to fix it!

- [ ] Check that your article includes the important details about the topic.

- [ ] Confirm that you describe a change related to your topic.

- [ ] Make sure your headline reflects your article.

- [ ] Make any final changes to your article on paper.

Share Your Project

Now's the time for your team to share your newspaper article with the rest of the class.

- [ ] Share your article with classmates or post on a class wall.

- [ ] Encourage classmates to ask questions about your article.

- [ ] Respond to questions in writing or orally.

Reflect on Your Project

Think about the work you did in this chapter and on your project.
Use the questions below to help guide your thoughts.

1. Why did you select the topic for your newspaper article? _____

_____

2. How did you conduct your research? _____

_____

3. Is there anything you would do differently next time? _____

_____

Chapter Connections

Use pictures, words, or both to reflect on what you learned in this
chapter.

The most interesting thing I learned:

Something I learned from a classmate:

A connection I can make with my own life:

Chapter 4

The Midwest

ESSENTIAL **EQ** QUESTION

How Does the Midwest Reflect the Spirit of America?

In this chapter, you'll read about Native Americans who first lived in this region. You'll read about conflicts that occurred when settlers moved westward onto the same land. You will also read about how the climate and geography of the region led to the growth of industries. You'll then explore how the Midwest holds to many of its traditions while adapting to a modern economy.

Talk About It COLLABORATE

Discuss with a partner questions you have about the Midwest region. Think about the region's climate, geography, history, economy, and more. As you read and research, look for answers to your questions. Let's explore the Midwest!

Inquiry Project

Road Trip Through the Midwest

Work with a partner to plan a road trip to explore how the Midwest reflects the American spirit. Find and describe four or five interesting Midwest places to visit. Choose from locations of historical events, interesting geographic places, important centers for the economy, or homes of famous leaders. Map and describe your locations to finish your road trip plan.

Project Checklist

- ☐ **Choose** an area on which to focus. It could be the Great Lakes, a particular state, or several states close together.

- ☐ **Research** interesting events, places, people, or industries in the area you chose.

- ☐ **Decide** how to present your road trip. What type of presentation, using paper or a computer, will you create?

- ☐ **Write** a description of each place you chose for your trip.

- ☐ **Assemble** your final road trip plan, including visuals to help illustrate your trip.

My Research Plan

Write down any research questions you have that will help you plan your project. You can add questions as you carry out your research.

_____

_____

_____

Explore / Words

Complete this chapter's Word Rater.
Write notes as you learn more about each word.

alternative energy

My Notes

☐ Know It!

_____

☐ Heard It!

_____

☐ Don't Know It!

_____

assembly line

My Notes

☐ Know It!

_____

☐ Heard It!

_____

☐ Don't Know It!

_____

automation

My Notes

☐ Know It!

_____

☐ Heard It!

_____

☐ Don't Know It!

_____

discrimination

My Notes

☐ Know It!

_____

☐ Heard It!

_____

☐ Don't Know It!

_____

drainage

My Notes

☐ Know It!

_____

☐ Heard It!

_____

☐ Don't Know It!

_____

expedition

My Notes

☐ Know It!

☐ Heard It!

☐ Don't Know It!

_____

_____

_____

invasive

My Notes

☐ Know It!

☐ Heard It!

☐ Don't Know It!

_____

_____

_____

irrigation

My Notes

☐ Know It!

☐ Heard It!

☐ Don't Know It!

_____

_____

_____

prairie

My Notes

☐ Know It!

☐ Heard It!

☐ Don't Know It!

_____

_____

_____

reservation

My Notes

☐ Know It!

☐ Heard It!

☐ Don't Know It!

_____

_____

_____

Lesson 1

How Did the Midwest's Climate and Geography Affect Early Peoples?

Lesson Outcomes

What Am I Learning?

In this lesson, you're going to use your investigative skills to explore how the Midwest's climate and geography affected early peoples living there.

Why Am I Learning It?

Reading and talking about the Midwest's climate and geography will help you understand how these factors influenced the region's first inhabitants.

How Will I Know That I Learned It?

You will be able to explain how climate and geography affected the lives of early peoples in the Midwest.

Talk About It

COLLABORATE

Look closely at the picture. What physical features do you notice? Who lived there? How do you know?

The first people to live in the Midwest were Native Americans.

1 Inspect

Read Look at the title. What do you think this lesson will be about?

Underline what features characterize buffalo hide painting.

Circle the reasons buffalo hides were used.

My Notes

_____
_____
_____
_____
_____
_____
_____
_____
_____
_____
_____
_____
_____
_____

Buffalo Hide Paintings

Vast herds of bison lived on the Great Plains before the 1900s. These bison are often referred to as buffalo. Native Americans of the Plains relied on the buffalo. Women tanned the buffalo hides to make them smooth. The hides were used as tarps, teepees, blankets, and clothing. Each skin had a furry side and a smooth side. People wore robes with the fur against their bodies to protect them from the harsh winters.

Hides had uses other than warmth. Talented artists painted shapes and scenes in different colors on the smooth side of the robes. Women usually wore hides decorated with shapes and patterns. Men's robes often showed large scenes. Some robes featured warriors coming home after a raid. Others showed men riding horses.

Sick people wore hides painted with healing symbols they believed would help them get well again. Leaders and holy people had special hides that displayed their importance in the community. Holy men and women used the hides to communicate with the spirit world.

Some Plains peoples recorded their history on buffalo hide paintings. Leaders chose the most important event from the year, and artists added a picture to a hide to represent that event. Tribe members could identify the year they were born by the event shown on that hide. They called these hides "winter counts."

Native Americans painted scenes that told important stories on buffalo hides.

2 Find Evidence

Reread In what ways did buffalo hides help the Plains peoples?

Underline the differences between the ways men and women used hides.

3 Make Connections

Talk What was the purpose of "winter counts"?

Explore Ask and Answer Questions

We ask questions to get information. A question often begins with *who, what, where, when, why,* or *how.* To answer a question, look for details that support the answer you find.

1. **Ask a question using *who, what, where, when, why,* or *how.***
   When you read, pay attention to something you don't understand. Ask yourself a *W* question or a *how* question.

2. **Look for details in the text that would support your answer.**
   Look for details that support the topic or answer your question.

3. **Answer your question.**
   Use the details that you found to formulate an answer to your question.

 Based on the text you read, work with your class to complete the chart below.

Question	Supporting Details	Answer
Why did the Plains peoples paint buffalo hides?		

Investigate!

Read pages 184–193 in your Research Companion. Use your investigative skills to look for text evidence that provides supporting details to help you answer questions. This chart will help you organize your notes.

Question	Supporting Details	Answer
Why did Native Americans build mounds?		
How did physical features of the Midwest benefit early peoples?		
How do tornadoes, the lake effect, and the seasons affect the Midwest?		
What natural resources did the inhabitants of the Midwest use?		
Why were animals important to the Sioux?		

Think About It

Review

Review your research. Based on the information you have gathered, how did the physical features, climate, and natural resources of the Midwest affect early peoples living there?

Write About It

Write and Cite Evidence

In what ways did the physical features, climate, and natural resources of the Midwest help and hurt early peoples? Use facts from the text to explain your response.

_____

_____

_____

_____

Explain

How do you think people today use the natural resources and adapt to the climate of the Midwest in similar and different ways from early peoples?

_____

_____

_____

_____

_____

_____

Talk About It

Explain

In a small group, talk about how the lives of early peoples in the Midwest differ from the lives of people today.

graphy

Connect to the

Pull It Together

How does the Midwest's climate and geography help define its spirit?

_____

_____

_____

_____

_____

_____

Inquiry Project Notes

_____

_____

_____

_____

_____

Why Did Different Peoples Move To and Through the Midwest?

Lesson Outcomes

What Am I Learning?

In this lesson, you're going to use your investigative skills to explore what influenced the movement of different groups of people to and through the Midwest during the western expansion of the United States.

Why Am I Learning It?

Reading and talking about what influenced the movement of different groups of people to and through the Midwest will help you learn more about how the United States developed.

How Will I Know That I Learned It?

You will be able to explain what influenced early settlers to move to and through the Midwest.

Talk About It

COLLABORATE

Look closely at the historical drawing. Where are these people? What are they doing? What details give you clues about their location and actions?

Sacagawea guided Lewis and Clark on their journey through the Louisiana Territory.

1 Inspect

Read Look at the title. What do you think this text will be about?

Circle important dates in the text.

Underline clues that signal ways the Corps of Discovery carried out its mission.

My Notes

_____

_____

_____

_____

_____

_____

_____

_____

_____

_____

_____

_____

_____

_____

The Lewis and Clark Expedition

In 1803, President Thomas Jefferson sent Meriwether Lewis to lead an **expedition** into land west of the Mississippi River. This land was known as the Louisiana Territory. Jefferson wanted Lewis to make contact with the Native Americans who lived there and to find a water route to the Pacific Ocean. Jefferson also asked Lewis to document the expedition's findings. Lewis asked William Clark to help lead the members of the expedition, which was called the Corps of Discovery.

The expedition started in 1804. The group traveled from St. Louis, Missouri, to the Pacific coast and back. Lewis and Clark kept detailed journals of their trip. The journals documented their daily activities and interactions with Native Americans.

In April 1805, Lewis sent President Jefferson a letter from Fort Mandan in present-day North Dakota. Lewis also sent several boxes and trunks that included animal skins, bones, plants, and dirt samples, along with an invoice, or list, of these items.

The Corps of Discovery did not find a water route to the Pacific, but Lewis and Clark found many other things. The journals described at least 120 mammals, birds, reptiles, and fish that Europeans had never seen. They also listed at least 182 plant species. A map of the Missouri River, drawn in the journals, was the most accurate map of the river available until the 1840s. The information they provided and the relationships they made helped lay the groundwork for Americans to move and settle west of the Mississippi.

Dear Sir.

Herewith inclosed you will receive an invoice of certain articles, which I have forwarded to you from this place. among other articles, you will observe by reference to the invoice, 67. specimens of earths, salts and minerals; and 60 specimens of plants: these are accompanyed by their rispective labels expressing the days on which obtained, places where found, and also their virtues and properties when known. by means of these labels, reference may be made to the Chart of the Missouri forwarded to the Secretary at War, on which, the encampment of each day has been carefully marked; thus the places at which these specimens have been obtained may be easily pointed out, or again found, should any of them prove valuable to the community on further investegation.

—from a letter written by Meriwether Lewis, 1805

Lewis and Clark wrote notes and made sketches on their journey.

2 Find Evidence

Reread How did the Corps of Discovery carry out President Jefferson's goals for the expedition?

3 Make Connections

Talk What were the results of the Lewis and Clark expedition? Which result of their expedition do you think was most important?

COLLABORATE

Explore Chronology

Chronology is the order in which events happen. When you examine a text, think about the chronology of the events described to help you understand how these events are related.

To track chronology:

1. **Read the text all the way through.**
    This will help you understand what the text is about.

2. **Reread the text and watch for specific dates and signal words. Are events in the text presented in chronological order?**
    Look for dates and for signal words such as *before* and *after*.

3. **Examine maps and other images.**
    Read the titles, captions, and labels of images and maps. Are any key facts presented? Decide how that information fits into the chronology of the text.

4. **Connect information to find results.**
    Review key facts and dates. How can connecting information by putting it in order help you understand the chronology of Lewis and Clark's expedition?

Based on the text you read, work with your class to complete the chart below.

Event	Date	Result
President Thomas Jefferson hires Meriwether Lewis to lead an expedition into the Louisiana Territory.		

Investigate!

Read pages 194–203 in your Research Companion. Use your investigative skills to look for text evidence that tells you what events influenced the movement of early Americans to and through the Midwest. Look for the result of those influences.

Event	Date	Result

Think About It

Review Your Research

Review your research. What events do you think most influenced the movement of early settlers to the Midwest? Explain your thinking.

Write About It

Explain

How did government actions encourage people to move to the Midwest in the mid-1800s?

_____

_____

_____

_____

_____

Write and Cite Evidence

How did the Homestead Act influence the movement of different peoples in the Midwest? Use the text to explain your response.

_____

_____

_____

_____

_____

_____

Talk About It

Explain

Share your response with a group. Together, discuss how government action influenced the movement of people in the Midwest.

History

Connect to the

Pull It Together

How do the events that led to the settlement of the Midwest reflect the spirit and changing of America in the 1800s?

_____

_____

_____

_____

_____

Inquiry Project Notes

_____

_____

_____

_____

_____

Lesson 3

How Did Lakes and Rivers Contribute to the Industrial Growth of the Midwest?

Lesson Outcomes

What Am I Learning?
In this lesson, you're going to use your investigative skills to explore how lakes and rivers contributed to the industrial growth of the Midwest.

Why Am I Learning It?
Reading and talking about how lakes and rivers helped industrial growth will help you learn more about the history of the major cities in the Midwest.

How Will I Know That I Learned It?
You will be able to explain how being located near the Great Lakes and other waterways helped major cities in the Midwest grow.

Talk About It
COLLABORATE

Look closely at the picture. What do you notice about the buildings? What kinds of transportation do you see?

Cities in the Midwest like Detroit, Michigan, grew as more businesses and factories opened.

The Great Migration

Throughout much of the 1900s, laws in the South allowed **discrimination** against African Americans. For example, African Americans could not go to the same schools as whites or sit near white people in public places. In addition, economic conditions for African Americans in the South were poor due to sharecropping and a struggling farm economy.

During World War I, many Americans joined the army. Northern factories needed workers to help with war production. They placed ads in newspapers in the South looking for workers. Large numbers of African Americans began moving to northern cities to take these jobs and to escape unfair laws. Many African Americans found jobs in northern factories. However, many of the jobs were difficult and unsafe. African Americans also faced discrimination in the North and the West.

About 6 million African Americans migrated north and west between 1910 and 1970 looking for a better life. The African American population in Chicago, Detroit, Philadelphia, and New York City grew rapidly between 1910 and 1940. In the 1940s, many African Americans moved to cities in the West, including Los Angeles, San Francisco, and Oakland. This movement of people would change America.

African Americans from the South moved to cities in the North during the Great Migration, looking for job opportunities.

2 Find Evidence

Reread Which words helped you identify problems African Americans were having?

Underline problems African Americans faced.

3 Make Connections

Talk Why did African Americans began moving to northern cities?

COLLABORATE

Explore Problem and Solution

Texts can be structured around a **problem** and the **solution** to that problem. The beginning of the text will describe the problem. The text that follows will describe a solution. The solution can be something that has already fixed the problem or something the writer is proposing could fix the problem.

To understand problem and solution:

1. **Read the text all the way through.**
   This will help you understand what the text is about.

2. **Look for an issue or problem being described.**
   Are there words that indicate a problem, such as *challenge* or *struggle*?

3. **Identify how the issue is resolved or the challenge overcome.**
   What did the person or group of people who were facing the challenge do to deal with the problem?

4. **Find a relationship between the solution and the problem.**
   Ask yourself if the people's actions solved the problem described at the beginning.

Based on the text you read, work with your class to complete the chart below.

Who?	Problem	Solution
African Americans living in the South		

Investigate!

Read pages 204–213 in your Research Companion. Use your investigative skills to look for text evidence that tells you about people who faced problems and how those people tried to solve the problems. This chart will help you organize your notes.

Who?	Problem	Solution
People of Chicago in 1871		

Think About It

Review Your Research
Based on the information you have gathered, why did people move to cities near the Great Lakes?

Write About It

Define
What are the Great Lakes?

_____

_____

_____

_____

_____

_____

_____

Write and Cite Evidence
Why did different people move to cities near the Great Lakes? Use facts from the text to explain your response.

_____

_____

_____

_____

_____

_____

_____

_____

Talk About It

Explain

Share your response with a partner. Together, discuss why the cities in the Midwest grew quickly during the late 1800s and early 1900s.

Connect to the

Pull It Together

Name three ways the growth of cities in the Midwest reflect the spirit of America.

_____

_____

_____

_____

_____

_____

_____

_____

Inquiry Project Notes

_____

_____

_____

_____

How Does the Midwest Honor Its Roots While Growing in a Modern Economy?

Lesson Outcomes

What Am I Learning?

In this lesson, you're going to use your investigative skills to explore how the Midwest has adapted in the modern economy, while staying connected to its roots.

Why Am I Learning It?

Reading and talking about changes in traditional Midwestern industries will help you understand the Midwest's role in the modern economy.

How Will I Know That I Learned It?

You will be able to describe the important changes in the Midwest and how Midwesterners addressed problems of growing in the modern economy while staying connected to the past.

Talk About It   COLLABORATE

Look at the picture. What details in this photo show modern innovation? What details show a connection to the past? How can you tell?

Mount Rushmore is the most popular attraction in South Dakota.

1 Inspect

Read Read the text and Primary Source feature. What does Gutzon Borglum's writing suggest about why the monument at Mount Rushmore was built?

- **Circle** words and phrases you don't know.
- **Underline** details that help you answer the questions *Who*, *What*, *Where*, *When*, or *Why*.
- **Discuss** with a partner some problems builders faced while making the monument.

My Notes

_____
_____
_____
_____
_____
_____
_____
_____
_____
_____

Building Mount Rushmore

In the Black Hills of South Dakota, the carved images of four American presidents look out from the side of Mount Rushmore. South Dakota's state historian wanted to promote tourism in his state while honoring American history. In 1924, he asked a famous sculptor, Gutzon Borglum, to create a design that would match the scale of the mountain.

Borglum planned to honor four American presidents he thought best stood for democracy. He chose George Washington, Thomas Jefferson, Abraham Lincoln, and Theodore Roosevelt. Drilling began in 1927. Workers used dynamite to blast out large sections of the mountain. Jackhammers and chisels carved the features of the faces.

The project nearly ended during the Great Depression. President Franklin D. Roosevelt provided federal funding to keep the builders working. He also created the Civilian Conservation Corps. This program helped support the project by building camps and clearing rubble for the carvers. More than 400 men and women worked at the site during the Great Depression. Work ended in 1941, shortly after Gutzon Borglum died.

Today, about 3 million tourists visit the Mount Rushmore National Memorial each year. It helps the area's economy by providing jobs and encouraging tourism.

Not everyone views the monument the same way. To the Sioux, Mount Rushmore represents land taken from them in a broken treaty. The Black Hills are also a sacred site for the Sioux.

In Their Words. . . Gutzon Borglum

"The purpose of the memorial is to communicate the founding, expansion, preservation, and unification of the United States with colossal statues of Washington, Jefferson, Lincoln, and Theodore Roosevelt."

—Gutzon Borglum, from the Foreword of the Mount Rushmore National Memorial booklet, 1930

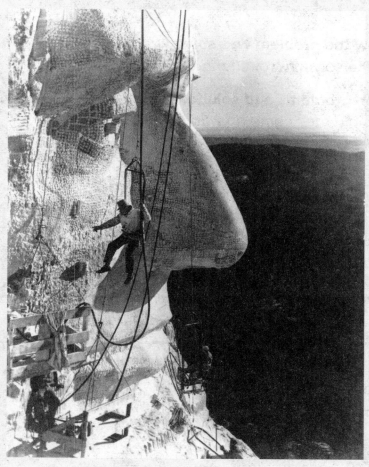

Workers on Mount Rushmore faced dangerous conditions as they added details to the faces of the presidents.

2 Find Evidence

Reread What does the text suggest about the purpose of the memorial at Mount Rushmore? What benefits did building the memorial bring? What does Mount Rushmore mean to different groups?

3 Make Connections

Talk How did Gutzon Borglum describe his purpose for the monument? How has the monument helped his vision endure?

COLLABORATE

Explore Problem and Solution

A **problem** is an issue that causes difficulty, trouble, or harm.

A **solution** is something that can be done to fix or overcome a problem.

To find problems and solutions as you read:

1. **Read the text all the way through.**
   This will help you understand what the text is about.

2. **Look for details that tell what the problem is.**
   Look for words or phrases that indicate a need for change, such as *difficulty* or *struggle*.

3. **Look for details that tell how the problem was solved.**
   Look for words or phrases like *solve*, *fix*, or *change*.

4. **Make a connection between problems and solutions.**
   Ask yourself, *What solutions did they come up with to solve these problems?*

Based on the text you read, work with your class to complete the chart below.

Problem	Solution
People of South Dakota needed a way to encourage tourists to visit their state.	

Investigate!

Read pages 214–221 in your Research Companion. Use your investigative skills to look for text evidence that tells you about the Midwest's challenges with growth in the modern economy and the solutions Midwesterners came up with. This chart will help you organize your notes.

Problem	Solution

Think About It

Review

Look back over your research about problems and solutions in the Midwest. How did innovation play a role?

Write About It

Write an Advertisement

Create an advertisement to get people to visit a city in the Midwest. Share some ways to experience the industrial and agricultural history of the Midwest, and describe new innovations a visitor might encounter. Support your advertisement with details from the text. Sketch or describe a graphic to go with your ad.

_____

_____

_____

_____

_____

Talk About It

Compare Advertisements

Compare your advertisement with a partner's advertisement. Afterwards, give your partner feedback. How persuasive is his or her advertisement? Which feature of the Midwest did the ad make you want to see?

onomics

Connect to the

Consider Problems and Solutions

Think about some of the problems and solutions you wrote about in your research. What are some solutions you think would help the Midwest continue to grow in the modern economy? How does this reflect the spirit of America?

_____

_____

_____

_____

_____

Inquiry Project Notes

_____

_____

_____

_____

_____

Lesson 5

How Does the Midwest Solve Problems We All Share?

Lesson Outcomes

What Am I Learning?

In this lesson, you are going to use your investigative skills to explore ways Midwesterners today are contributing to solve global problems.

Why Am I Learning It?

Reading and talking about these contributions will help you understand the importance of the Midwest as a region.

How Will I Know That I Learned It?

You will be able to make conclusions about the contributions of the Midwest and how they affect global conditions.

Talk About It

COLLABORATE

Look closely at the picture. What resources do you see? How do you think human activities affect these resources?

Some species of carp jump into the air when disturbed by boat motors.

Carp Species Threaten the Great Lakes

1 Inspect

Read Look at the title. What does it suggest about the topic?

- **Circle** words and phrases you don't know.
- **Underline** words, phrases, or sentences that help you understand what problem Midwesterners are trying to solve.
- **Discuss** with a partner the ways Asian carp are affecting Midwestern waterways.

My Notes

_____
_____
_____
_____
_____
_____
_____
_____
_____
_____
_____
_____

The waterways of the Midwest are important resources, especially the Great Lakes. They are used for trade and recreation. They are also vital to the environment. Like all concerned global citizens, Midwesterners have to take measures to keep resources such as the Great Lakes healthy.

Asian carp are large fish that harm waterways. They are **invasive** species. Invasive means the species spread and threaten native wildlife. As Asian carp populations take over rivers and lakes, they eat up all the food. Native fish starve and die off, which harms the freshwater environment.

The carp also pose a risk for humans. Some carp can grow up to 60 pounds and jump more than five feet in the air when disturbed by boat motors. They can cause serious injuries to boaters.

The first Asian carp were brought to fish hatcheries in the southeastern United States nearly 50 years ago. Some fish escaped during floods and started swimming up the Mississippi River.

If Asian carp continue to travel up rivers in the Midwest, they could threaten the Great Lakes. This is a critical concern for Midwestern governments and environmental agencies. Protective measures, such as electric barriers in dams and rivers, prevent Asian carp from entering the lakes. Environmental groups continually check fish populations in the Great Lakes. They are protecting the future of Midwestern waterways.

Asian Carp Barriers

Electric barriers in Midwestern rivers keep Asian carp from entering the Great Lakes.

2 Find Evidence

Reread What problem do Asian carp cause in the Midwest? What are some ways Midwesterners are trying to solve this problem?

3 Make Connections

Talk What role are Midwesterners playing in preventing the spread of invasive species? What do you think would happen if the carp spread into the Great Lakes?

COLLABORATE

Explore Details to Draw Conclusions

The **details** in a text and what you already know help you come to a **conclusion**. A conclusion is a decision or judgment. Sometimes a conclusion is an important idea, fact, or answer to a question.

To find the details that lead to a conclusion:

1. **Read the text all the way through to get an overall understanding.**

2. **Identify the author's important details or ideas.**

3. **Look for ways that the important details are related.**
   Ask yourself, *Why is the author telling me this?*

4. **Think about what you already know about the topic.**

5. **Put all the details and your prior knowledge together.**
   Ask yourself, *What conclusion, or judgment, can I make from this information?*

COLLABORATE

How are Midwesterners contributing as global citizens by protecting the Great Lakes? Based on the text you read, work with your class to complete the chart below.

Detail
Asian carp are invasive species threatening Midwestern waterways.

↓

Detail

↓

Conclusion

Investigate!

Read pages 222–229 in your Research Companion. Use your investigative skills to identify details that support the conclusion that Midwesterners contribute as global citizens. This chart will help you organize your notes.

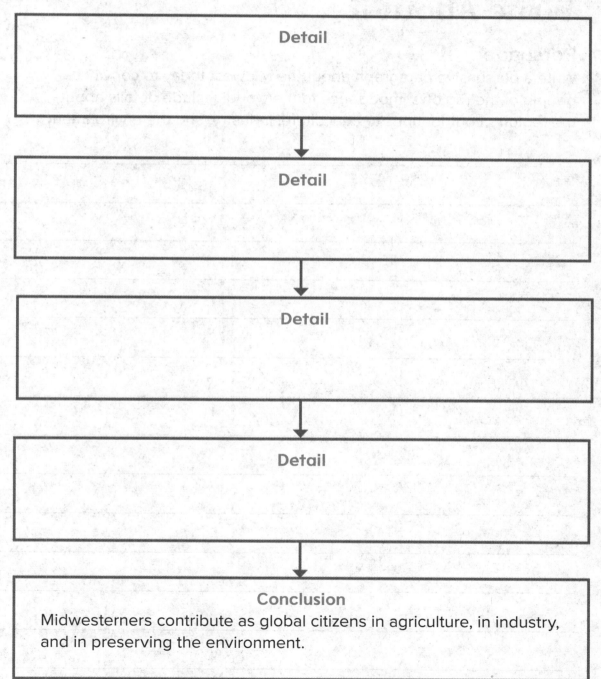

Detail

Detail

Detail

Detail

Conclusion

Midwesterners contribute as global citizens in agriculture, in industry, and in preserving the environment.

Think About It

Draw Conclusions

Review your research. Based on the information you have collected, what choices have Midwesterners made that show they are trying to be good global citizens?

Write About It

Persuade

Write a persuasive paragraph about the Midwest today to convince people of the region's importance to the world. Include details about the region's contributions to agriculture, industry, and the environment.

_____

_____

_____

_____

_____

_____

_____

_____

_____

_____

_____

_____

Talk About It

Compare

Share your persuasive paragraph with a classmate. Compare and contrast information you included in your paragraphs. Discuss which details best convince the reader of the Midwest's importance and why you think so.

Citizenship

Connect to the

Pull It Together

Review your conclusions about how Midwesterners contribute as global citizens. How do these contributions reflect the spirit of America?

_____

_____

_____

_____

_____

_____

_____

Inquiry Project Notes

_____

_____

_____

How Does the Midwest Reflect the Spirit of America?

Inquiry Project

Road Trip Through the Midwest

Now complete your Road Trip Through the Midwest project with a checklist, and then present it to your class.

Complete Your Project

Use this checklist to wrap up your project.

☐ Check that your research and sources are accurate.

☐ Change a place to visit if you have too little information.

☐ Add any information about locations that you might have from your own personal experience or background knowledge.

☐ Practice with your partner what you want to say when you present to the class.

Share Your Project

Now's the time for you and your partner to present your work to the class.

☐ Remember to speak naturally and make eye contact with the class.

☐ Share an interesting feature before giving details.

☐ Start from the first location on the map and move in order, based on the points you marked on the map.

☐ Ask if anyone in the class has personal ties in the area to get feedback.

Reflect on Your Project

Think about the work you did in this chapter and on your project. Use the questions below to help guide your thoughts.

1. How did you and your partner select places to "visit" in the Road Trip Through the Midwest project? _____

_____

2. Did you make sure that your sources were reliable? Did you show the key events, people, places, or industries of your area? _____

_____

3. Is there anything you would do differently next time? _____

_____

Chapter Connections

Use pictures, words, or both to reflect on what you learned in this chapter.

The most interesting thing I learned:

Something I learned from a classmate:

A connection I can make with my own life:

Our Class Project to Save Salt Creek

CHARACTERS

Ms. Smith	Narrator	Raul
Kaitlyn	Jacob	Entire Class
Elizabeth		

Ms. Smith: This week, we've been discussing why it's important to protect our environment. Tomorrow we're going to break into teams, and each team is going to do a project about protecting the environment. Tonight, I want you to think about a project you and your teammates can work on together.

Kaitlyn: Oh, no. More homework!

Elizabeth: How are a few kids supposed to protect the environment?

Narrator: After school, Jacob and Raul walk home along Salt Creek after baseball practice.

Jacob: Are those old bottles and food wrappers near the creek?

Raul: Yeah, and check out that broken window over there.

Jacob: How did all this junk get here?

Raul:
People use the creek as a dumping ground. They just dump junk here and bring more all the time. They have turned the creek into a garbage dump. What a shame! People used to enjoy the creek a lot more. My uncle told me that he used to go fishing here. He'd catch bass and pike and bring them home for my grandma to cook.

Jacob: If there are any fish in that polluted water now, I wouldn't want to eat them. This place stinks.

Narrator: The boys soon arrive in front of Raul's house.

Jacob: Can we be on the same team in Ms. Smith's class?

Raul: Sure. Let's try to think of a great idea for the project!

Narrator: The next day, Ms. Smith organizes the class into teams. Raul, Jacob, Kaitlyn, and Elizabeth are on the same team.

Kaitlyn: Okay, has anybody thought of a good project yet?

Raul: Jacob and I talked about our ideas yesterday. I think we should clean up Salt Creek so people can use it for fishing again.

Elizabeth: Wow, that's a lot of work!

Kaitlyn: Let's go look at the creek before we jump into this project.

Narrator: After school, Kaitlyn, Elizabeth, Jacob, and Raul visit the creek. Raul hands everyone large garbage bags and gloves. The kids fill the bags with bottles, tires, cans, food wrappers, paper, and other trash.

Kaitlyn: We've only covered one small area. How are we going to be able to clean up the whole creek?

Elizabeth: I've got an idea. Why don't we ask Ms. Smith if the entire class can work on this project?

Raul: Now you're thinking!

Narrator: The next day the team tells the class about Salt Creek and Raul's idea to clean it up.

Ms. Smith: What do you think, class? Raise your hand if you'd like to do this project.

Narrator: Everyone's hand went up. Soon the entire class was working on clearing garbage around the creek. Every time they showed up, though, they would see new garbage. Back in class, the group talked about what to do about this problem.

Kaitlyn: Why do some people treat the creek like a garbage dump? The people who litter there should be punished.

Entire Class: We should put up a sign telling people not to dump garbage here.

Ms. Smith: These are both good ideas. Let's write to the city council and see if they can do anything to support our project.

Narrator: Soon a sign was posted near the creek. It said, "NO DUMPING AT THE CREEK. MINIMUM FINE $250." But there was still more to do to protect the creek.

Ms. Smith: Class, you've done a great job so far. But we still need to do something about the garbage in the creek that we can't pick up.

Entire Class: What's the kind of garbage that we can't pick up?

Ms. Smith: When people wash their cars or change the oil in their car, sometimes the dirty water or oil goes down the drain in the street. The rain then carries that polluted water into Salt Creek.

Entire Class: How are we supposed to stop people from getting dirty water in the street drains?

Kaitlyn: Where my cousin lives, they have signs on the drains to remind people that whatever goes down them will end up in the river.

Narrator: The class painted signs on storm drains that led to the creek. "Don't Dump Waste. Drains to Stream."

Ms. Smith: Class, I have an announcement to make. You did an amazing job on this project. What a great accomplishment!

Write About It

Write your own Reader's Theater play about an environmental project.

Chapter 5

The Southwest

How Does the Southwest Reflect Its Diverse Past and Unique Environment?

In this chapter, you'll read about the environment of the Southwest. You'll read about how early peoples lived in this region and how the arrival of the Spanish affected their lives. You will also read why many settlers moved to the Southwest and about the industries that became important then and now. Finally, you will examine how the Southwest provides a launching pad for science and discovery.

Talk About It

Discuss with your partner questions you have about the region's climate and geography. Think about why these properties drove people in and out of the Southwest. As you research, look for answers to your questions.

Inquiry Project

One of a Kind

Work with a partner to plan a TV show about what makes the Southwest one of a kind among regions in the United States. Write a description of what your show would be called and what it would be about. Tell the time period and Southwest location of your show. Describe the characters and events that would take place on your TV show. Create visuals to reflect the events and location. Present your show idea to the class.

Project Checklist

☐ **Choose** a time period and Southwest location for your show.

☐ **Research** events, geography, and climate from this time period and location.

☐ **Write** a description of your TV show — the characters, time period, location, and events of your show.

☐ **Choose** a name for your show.

☐ **Add** some visuals to your show description to reflect the events and location of your TV show.

My Research Plan

Write down any research questions you have that will help you plan your project. You can add questions as you carry out your research.

_____

_____

_____

_____

_____

Explore Words

Complete this chapter's Word Rater.
Write notes as you learn more about each word.

aerospace
- ☐ Know It!
- ☐ Heard It!
- ☐ Don't Know It!

My Notes

_____

_____

_____

annex
- ☐ Know It!
- ☐ Heard It!
- ☐ Don't Know It!

My Notes

_____

_____

_____

arroyo
- ☐ Know It!
- ☐ Heard It!
- ☐ Don't Know It!

My Notes

_____

_____

_____

butte
- ☐ Know It!
- ☐ Heard It!
- ☐ Don't Know It!

My Notes

_____

_____

_____

experiment
- ☐ Know It!
- ☐ Heard It!
- ☐ Don't Know It!

My Notes

_____

_____

_____

geometric

My Notes

☐ **Know It!**

☐ **Heard It!**

☐ **Don't Know It!**

_____

_____

_____

interstate

My Notes

☐ **Know It!**

☐ **Heard It!**

☐ **Don't Know It!**

_____

_____

_____

mission

My Notes

☐ **Know It!**

☐ **Heard It!**

☐ **Don't Know It!**

_____

_____

_____

presidio

My Notes

☐ **Know It!**

☐ **Heard It!**

☐ **Don't Know It!**

_____

_____

_____

sovereign

My Notes

☐ **Know It!**

☐ **Heard It!**

☐ **Don't Know It!**

_____

_____

_____

Lesson 1

How Did Early Peoples Cope With the Harsh Environment of the Southwest?

Lesson Outcomes

What Am I Learning?

In this lesson, you're going to use your investigative skills to explore how the harsh environment of the Southwest was difficult for the early people who settled there.

Why Am I Learning It?

Reading and talking about the land and climate of the Southwest will help you learn about how early people adapted to their environments.

How Will I Know That I Learned It?

You will be able to explain what the challenges were and how people overcame them.

Talk About It

COLLABORATE

Look closely at the picture. What does the picture show? When do you think people lived here? How do you know?

Dwellings were built into the sides of cliffs in the Southwest.

1 Inspect

Look closely at the picture. What do you think this page will be about?

- **Circle** the paws and tail of the animal in the picture.
- **Identify** clues that tell you:

  What animal is depicted in the picture?

  Is the animal calm or angry?

- **Discuss** your answers with a partner.

My Notes

_____

_____

_____

_____

_____

_____

_____

_____

_____

_____

_____

Petroglyphs of the Southwest

Throughout the Southwest region, pictures called petroglyphs can be found on canyon walls and in caves. These drawings are of snakes, sheep, elk, and other interesting animals, shapes, and figures. Some were drawn as separate images. Others were grouped together to create a scene. Ancient peoples chipped or ground them into the rock walls. Most historians believe a group called the Ancient Puebloans created them between A.D. 600 and A.D. 1200. However, some say the petroglyphs may have been carved as early as 300 B.C.

No one is exactly sure what the petroglyphs mean. They may be road signs that told travelers where to find water, or they may be the historical records of ancient people. Historians are sure that petroglyphs are not just doodles because they took a long time to carve. Pecking, chipping, and etching pictures into rock is difficult and careful work. Some of these carvings are very detailed. The artists had to be very skilled to create their art.

In addition to petroglyphs, ancient paintings have been found in the Southwest. These paintings on rocks or other outdoor surfaces are called pictographs. Ancient peoples made paints from minerals, plants, or ashes. Most pictographs faded away a long time ago. Those that still can be seen are in caves or other places that are protected from the weather.

This mountain lion petroglyph was found at the Petrified Forest National Park in Arizona.

2 Find Evidence

Reread What does the text suggest about how petroglyphs were created? What mystery still surrounds these petroglyphs?

3 Make Connections

Talk When do you think this petroglyph was created? What do you think the creator is trying to show? Explain why you think so.

COLLABORATE

Explore Compare and Contrast

When you **compare and contrast,** you explain how two or more things are alike and different. Comparing and contrasting helps you identify similarities and differences among events and ideas.

1. **Read the text once all the way through.**
   This will help you understand what the text is about.

2. **Look for key facts and details that show differences about two topics.**
   How are the topics different? Which facts and details show these differences?

3. **Look for key facts and details that show similarities about the topics.**
   How are the topics the same? Which facts and details show these similarities?

4. **Use key facts or details to compare and contrast the topics.**
   Use important facts and details to explain how the topics are alike and how they are different.

 Based on the text you read, work with your class to complete the chart below.

Compare and Contrast Petroglyphs and Pictographs	
Similar	Different

Investigate!

Read pages 242–251 in your Research Companion. Use your investigative skills to compare and contrast the geographic regions of the Southwest, including the plants, animals, and Native American groups that live or have lived there.

Compare the Gulf Coastal Plain and Desert Areas of the Southwest	
Similar	**Different**

Compare Hopi and Navajo Groups	
Similar	**Different**

Think About It

Research
Review your research. Based on the information you gathered, how do you think people in the Southwest survived the harsh environment?

Write About It

Write and Cite Evidence
From what you read in this lesson, tell how the Native Americans of the Southwest adapted to the region's unique environment.

_____

_____

_____

_____

_____

_____

_____

_____

_____

_____

_____

_____

_____

_____

Talk About It

Compare and Contrast

Exchange notes on how early Native peoples adjusted to living in the Southwest. Compare and contrast with how you think citizens today adapt to the Southwest.

graphy

Connect to the

Pull It Together

How does the Southwest region's environment make it unique?

_____

_____

_____

_____

_____

_____

_____

_____

_____

_____

Inquiry Project Notes

_____

_____

_____

What Impact Did the Arrival of the Spanish Have on the Southwest?

Lesson Outcomes

What Am I Learning?

In this lesson, you're going to use your investigative skills to explore the impact the arrival of the Spanish had on the Southwest region of the United States.

Why Am I Learning It?

Reading and talking about the arrival of the Spanish will help you learn more about the history of the Southwest.

How Will I Know That I Learned It?

You will be able to explain the impact the Spanish had on the Southwest.

Talk About It

COLLABORATE

Look closely at the map. What looks the same as a modern map? What is different?

Spanish conquistadors who arrived in the Southwest explored the land and searched for gold.

1 Inspect

Read Look at the title. What does it suggest the text will be about?

Circle words or phrases you don't know.

Underline key details that help you understand:

- Who were conquistadors?
- Why did the Spanish conquistadors come to the Americas?
- How did Cortés's goals change once he arrived in North America?

My Notes

_____

_____

_____

_____

_____

_____

_____

_____

_____

_____

The Establishment of New Spain

When Christopher Columbus sailed across the Atlantic, he hoped to find a new sea route to Asia. Instead he found lands and people that he had not expected to find. Other Spanish explorers called *conquistadors* soon followed Columbus across the ocean. These conquistadors were Spanish soldiers who took the lands that they came across by force. They claimed these lands for Spain.

One of these conquistadors was Hernán Cortés (er-NAHN kor-TEHZ). Cortés knew about the land Columbus had found. Cortés left Spain in 1504 and sailed to the Western Hemisphere to explore the territory himself. Cortés hoped to find gold.

Cortés reached the city of Tenochtitlán (tay-nohch-teet-LAHN) in November 1519. This city was the capital of the Aztec empire. The ruler of the Aztec people was Montezuma II. He greeted Cortés with presents. Eventually, Cortés defeated the Aztec and took possession of their land. The land of the Aztec and other nearby territories captured by the Spanish became the colony of New Spain.

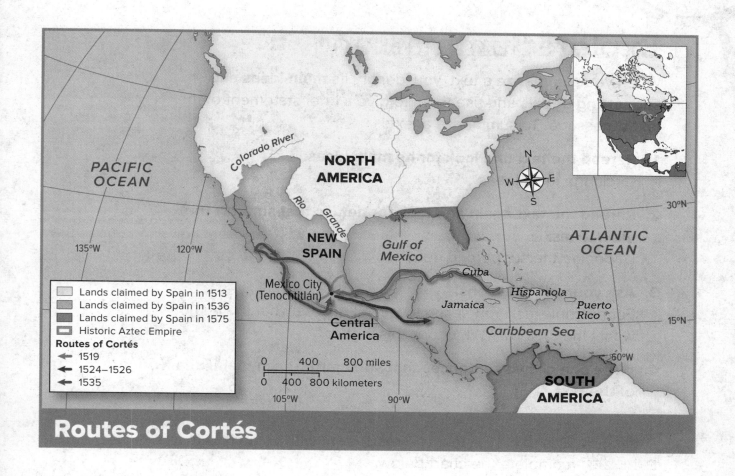

Routes of Cortés

2 Find Evidence

Reread How does the map help you understand the text?

Underline the names of important places in the text that are shown in the map.

3 Make Connections

Talk How did the goals of the Spanish explorers change as they learned more from their explorations? How did Spanish exploration affect North America?

COLLABORATE

Explore Summarizing

When you **summarize** a text, you identify its **main ideas** and **supporting details** and use them to give a brief statement of the text's message. To summarize a text:

1. **Reread the text and look for its main ideas.**
   Circle the main ideas.

2. **Reread the text again and look for details that support the main ideas.**
   Underline the supporting details.

3. **Ask yourself questions.**
   For example, ask yourself, "How can I restate what the author wants me to know? Why does this matter?"

4. **Write one or two sentences that summarize each main idea of the text.**

COLLABORATE

Based on the text you read, work with your class to complete the chart below.

> **Main Idea** The Establishment of New Spain
>
> **Detail 1** _____
>
> _____
>
> **Detail 2** _____
>
> _____

↓

> **Summary** _____
>
> _____
>
> _____
>
> _____

Investigate!

Read pages 252–261 in your Research Companion. Use your investigative skills to look for text evidence that tells you the most important details of what happened. This chart will help you organize your notes.

Main Idea The Spanish Mission System

   Detail 1

   Detail 2

Main Idea Impact of Missions on Native Americans

   Detail 1

   Detail 2

Main Idea Rancho Lifestyle

   Detail 1

   Detail 2

Summary

Think About It

Review your research. Based on the information you have gathered, how do you think the arrival of the Spanish impacted the Southwest?

Write About It

Define

What does *impacted* mean?

_____

Write and Cite Evidence

How did the arrival of the Spanish impact North America? Use facts from the texts to explain your response.

_____

_____

_____

_____

_____

_____

_____

_____

Talk About It

Explain

Share your response with a partner. Together discuss how your research showed the impact of the Spanish on North America.

History

Connect to the

Pull It Together

How does the Southwest today show Spain's impact on North America?

1. _____

_____

_____

2. _____

_____

_____

3. _____

_____

_____

Inquiry Project Notes

_____

_____

_____

_____

What Drove People In and Out of the Southwest?

Lesson Outcomes

What Am I Learning?

In this lesson, you're going to use your investigative skills to explore the events and opportunities that drove people in and out of the Southwest.

Why Am I Learning It?

Reading and talking about events in the Southwest will help you understand why some people came to the region and some people left the region.

How Will I Know That I Learned It?

You will be able to explain why some people were drawn to the Southwest, while others were driven out.

Talk About It

COLLABORATE

Look closely at the picture. What are the people in the picture doing? What reasons can you think of that might cause conflict between people?

The Battle of the Alamo took place in San Antonio, Texas, in 1836.

The Battle of the Alamo

1 Inspect

Read Look at the title. What does it suggest about the kind of text this will be?

- **Circle** words and phrases that you do not know.
- **Underline** important facts and details that answer the questions *Who*, *What*, *When*, *Where*, or *Why*.
- **Highlight** clues in the text that help you understand the reasons behind the conflict.

My Notes

_____

_____

_____

_____

_____

_____

_____

_____

_____

_____

_____

In 1836, Texas was part of Mexico. However, Texans who had migrated from the United States wanted independence from the Mexican government. This led to fighting between the Texans and the Mexican army.

The Alamo was an abandoned Spanish mission in San Antonio, Texas. About 200 Texans had set up a fort in the Alamo to hold off the Mexican troops. Mexican General Santa Anna surrounded the fort with thousands of Mexican soldiers. Santa Anna ordered the men inside the Alamo to surrender.

Alamo commander William Travis wrote a letter to Texas army general Sam Houston. Travis asked for more troops to come help. He promised to never surrender or retreat. Travis and his soldiers fought bravely, but in the end, every man was killed by the Mexican soldiers. However, his letter and actions had a tremendous impact on the Texas army. It gave them the determination to win the war for Texas independence a few months later.

In Their Words. . . William Travis

"I call on you in the name of Liberty, of patriotism and everything dear to the American character, to come to our aid, with all dispatch— The enemy is receiving reinforcements daily and will no doubt increase to three or four thousand in four or five days. If this call is neglected, I am determined to sustain myself as long as possible and die like a soldier who never forgets what is due to his own honor and that of his country—Victory or Death."

—William Travis's letter written from the Alamo to Sam Houston, February 14, 1836

The bravery of William Travis and the defenders of the Alamo is honored at this monument, the Alamo Cenotaph in San Antonio, Texas.

2 Find Evidence

Reread What was happening when William Travis sent his letter during the Battle of the Alamo? What does the letter say he plans to do? What words did he use to describe his determination?

3 Make Connections

Talk Discuss with a partner the results of William Travis's letter. What do you think he meant by "Victory or Death"? Did his letter have an effect on the outcome of the Texas Revolution?

COLLABORATE

Explore Chronology

Chronology is the order in which events happen. When you examine a text, think about the chronology of the events described to help you understand how they are related.

1. **Read the text once all the way through.**
   This will help you understand what the text is about.

2. **Watch for specific dates and signal words.**
   Are events in the text presented in chronological order? Look for dates and for signal words such as *before* and *after*.

3. **Examine maps and other images.**
   Read the titles, captions, and labels of images and maps. Are any key facts presented? Decide how that information fits into the chronology of the text.

4. **Connect information to find results.**
   Review the key facts. How can connecting information in chronological order help you understand the events that led people to enter and leave the Southwest?

 How did events at the Alamo affect people in the Southwest? Based on the text you read, work with your class to complete the chart below.

Event	Date	Result
William Travis writes a letter from the Battle of the Alamo, promising to never give up.		

Investigate!

Read pages 262–271 in your Research Companion. Use your investigative skills to identify the chronology of events that caused people to come into and go out of the Southwest. This chart will help you organize your notes.

Event	Date	Result
	↓	
	↓	
	↓	

Think About It

Identify Causes

Review your research. Based on the information you have gathered, what events do you think had the biggest impact on people moving to the Southwest? What events caused some to leave?

Write About It

Write a Newspaper Article

Imagine you are a journalist in the past who is reporting on changes in the Southwest. Choose one of the events you think influenced the growth of the Southwest. Use your research to write a short article about the event. Describe who, what, when, where, and why it happened, and how it affected people living in the Southwest.

_____

_____

_____

_____

_____

_____

_____

_____

_____

_____

Talk About It

Share

In a small group, share your newspaper articles. Discuss the events you chose for your articles. Identify the details that describe how the event affected people in the Southwest.

Connect to the

Pull It Together

Choose one of the events in the Southwest you studied in this lesson. Not all of the events had the same impact on all people. How do you think the event you chose affects different groups of people that live in the region today?

_____

_____

_____

_____

_____

_____

_____

_____

Inquiry Project Notes

_____

_____

_____

_____

Lesson 4

How Has the Past Influenced the Culture and Economy Today?

Lesson Outcomes

What Am I Learning?

In this lesson, you're going to use your investigative skills to explore the culture and economy in the Southwest.

Why Am I Learning It?

Reading and talking about the Southwest's unique contributions to culture will help you learn about this region's characteristics.

How Will I Know That I Learned It?

You will be able to describe key characteristics of the Southwest's economy and culture from the past to the present.

Talk About It

COLLABORATE

Look closely at the picture. What is happening? How does this activity contribute to the economy of the Southwest?

Oil fields are part of the landscape in Texas and Oklahoma.

1 Inspect

Predict Look at the heading and read the lesson question. What do you think this lesson will cover?

Circle important numbers related to the oil industry of Texas.

Highlight how the oil industry changed people's lives in Texas and throughout the world.

My Notes

_____
_____
_____
_____
_____
_____
_____
_____
_____
_____
_____

The Oil Industry in the Southwest

Oil drillers on Spindletop Hill near Beaumont, Texas, hit the jackpot on January 10, 1901. A giant geyser of oil exploded out of the earth. The Lucas Geyser, as it came to be called, blasted for nine days until workers could control it. The "gusher" produced about 100,000 barrels of oil per day for more than a year. This was the biggest oil strike in the world at that time. Eager fortune seekers flooded to the scene to drill their own wells. Beaumont's population ballooned from 10,000 to 50,000 people in a few months. The Texas oil boom was born, as was the modern oil industry.

Oil speculators invested money in setting up wells across Texas in the hopes of making a profit. Within a year, more than 1,500 oil companies opened. The cheap fuel made from the oil provided kerosene for lamps. Over time, oil was made into gasoline to power engines and machinery. Eventually, automobiles began using gasoline so the automoblie industry was linked to the oil industry. Products like petroleum jelly were invented from oil deposits.

The Texas oil industry developed throughout the 20th century. Oil was refined, or converted into a usable form, more efficiently. Chemical companies also opened in Texas. This Southwest state continues to dominate the oil industry in the United States today.

Beaumont, Texas, was the site of an oil strike in 1901.

2 Find Evidence

Summarize What happened on Spindletop Hill that made it important to history?

Underline how Texas's population changed before and after the start of the oil industry.

3 Make Connections

Talk How does the Spindletop discovery relate to modern life in the Southwest?

Explore Chronology

Putting events in order while you read, or identifying **chronology**, will help you understand the relationship between events.

1. **Read the text once all the way through.**
   To get an overall sense of what a text is about, read it all the way through without stopping.

2. **Reread a second time.**
   Ask yourself questions as you read a second time.

3. **Notice how the text is organized.**
   Look for clues that tell time order. Do you see dates or time order words such as *first, second, then, after,* or *finally*?

4. **Look at text features.**
   Do text features, such as headings, photos, or time lines, help you put events in order?

5. **Identify the most important events.**
   While reading, ask yourself what key facts about each event show that it was important to the Southwest's culture and economy.

COLLABORATE

Based on the text you read, work with your class to complete the chart below.

Event:

Key Facts:

Investigate!

Read pages 272–281 in your Research Companion. Use your investigative skills to look for text evidence that tells you when events happened and the order in which they happened. This chart will help you organize your notes.

Event:

Key Facts:

Event:

Key Facts:

Event:

Key Facts:

Event:

Key Facts:

Think About It

Review Your Research

Based on the information you have gathered, how has the past influenced the culture and economy of the Southwest today?

Write About It

Write and Cite Evidence

In what ways are the cuisine, art, and music of the Southwest unique? Use facts from the texts to explain your response.

_____

_____

_____

_____

_____

_____

_____

_____

_____

_____

_____

_____

_____

_____

Talk About It

Explain
With a partner, talk about the Southwest's past and its influence on the economy today. What industries are especially important?

Connect to the

Summarize
In what ways does the Southwest's history and environment affect how people in the region live today?

_____

_____

_____

_____

_____

_____

Inquiry Project Notes

_____

_____

_____

_____

_____

Lesson 5

How Does the Southwest Contribute to the Global Science Community?

Lesson Outcomes

What Am I Learning?

In this lesson, you are going to use your investigative skills to explore how the Southwest supports space research and exploration.

Why Am I Learning It?

Reading and talking about various efforts to learn about the universe helps us better understand Earth.

How Will I Know That I Learned It?

You will be able to explain the Southwest's contributions to space research and exploration.

Talk About It

COLLABORATE

Look closely at the picture. What is happening? Where do you think it is happening? Why might the location be important to the activity?

The wide-open spaces of the White Sands Missile Base in New Mexico provided an ideal location for space shuttle landings.

The Space Race

1 Inspect

Read the article. Why was the formation of NASA an important step in the space race?

Number the events in the space race.

Underline the accomplishments made by the United States in the space race.

My Notes

_____

_____

_____

_____

_____

_____

_____

_____

_____

_____

In 1957, the Soviet Union launched the first man-made satellite. It was called *Sputnik I*, and its launch marked the start of the space age. The Soviet Union's success worried and embarrassed the government of the United States. It meant that the United States had fallen behind in space exploration and technology.

To fix this, Congress established the National Aeronautics and Space Administration, or NASA, in 1958. As an arm of the federal government, NASA's responsibility is to coordinate U.S. activities in space. In 1961, NASA opened the Manned Spacecraft Center in Houston, Texas. The facility is now called the Lyndon B. Johnson Space Center. It is home to human space flight operations.

To further show the nation's commitment to the space program, President John F. Kennedy presented a challenge in 1961. He challenged the nation not only to go to the moon, but to do it before any other country, and to do it in just ten years. This effort continued the "space race."

On July 20, 1969, America's *Apollo 11* mission landed on the moon. *Apollo 11*'s astronauts became the first humans to walk on the moon. The United States took the lead in the space race—and lived up to President Kennedy's challenge.

In 1962, during a speech in Houston, Texas, President John F. Kennedy outlined America's goal of sending astronauts to the moon.

PRIMARY SOURCE

In Their Words... John F. Kennedy

"We choose to go to the moon in this decade and do the other things, not because they are easy, but because they are hard, because that goal will serve to organize and measure the best of our energies and skills, because that challenge is one that we are willing to accept, one we are unwilling to postpone, and one which we intend to win. . . . "

— *President John F. Kennedy, Rice University, September 12, 1962*

2 Find Evidence

Reread Why do you think the United States was so concerned about the Soviet Union's success with *Sputnik I*?

Circle words that tell you how members of the U.S. government felt.

Underline some things that the U.S. government did about it.

3 Make Connections

Talk What was President Kennedy's role in the space race? How did it affect NASA?

COLLABORATE

Explore Problem and Solution

Texts can be structured around a problem and the solution to the problem. The beginning of the text will describe the problem. The solution can be something that has already fixed the problem or something the writer is proposing could fix the problem.

To understand problem and solution:

1. **Read the text once all the way through.**
   This will help you understand what the text is about.

2. **Look for an issue or problem being described.**
   Are there words that indicate a problem, such as *challenge* or *hardship*?

3. **Identify how the issue is resolved or the challenge is overcome.**

4. **Find a relationship between the solution and the problem.** Did a person's or industry's actions solve the problem described at the beginning?

Based on the text you read, work with your class to complete the chart below.

Who	Problem	Solution
the United States		

Investigate!

Read pages 282–289 in your Research Companion. Use your investigative skills to look for text evidence that suggests problems and the solutions to those problems. This chart will help you organize your notes.

Who	Problem	Solution

Think About It

Review Your Research

Based on the information you have gathered, think about ways the Southwest contributes to the global science community.

Write About It

Write and Cite Evidence

How did the environment and other factors contribute to the space industry in the Southwest? What major accomplishments in space exploration happened in the Southwest? Use evidence from the texts to explain your answer.

_____

_____

_____

_____

_____

_____

_____

_____

_____

_____

_____

Talk About It

Explain

With a partner, explain how the Southwest contributes to the worldwide science community.

Connect to the

Summarize

How does the role of space exploration in the Southwest reflect its unique environment?

_____

_____

_____

_____

_____

Inquiry Project Notes

_____

_____

_____

_____

How Does the Southwest Reflect Its Diverse Past and Unique Environment?

ESSENTIAL EQ QUESTION

Inquiry Project

One of a Kind

Remember, for this project you will plan a TV show that explains why the Southwest is unique.

Complete Your Project

Use this checklist below to evaluate your project. If you left anything out, now's your chance to fix it!

☐ Complete your TV show description.

☐ Check that the show description reflects a unique part of the Southwest—key events, people, geography, and time period.

☐ Finish any visuals to go along with your TV show plan.

☐ Practice with your partner how to describe your show.

Share Your Project

Now's the time for you and your partner to present your work to the class. Introduce your TV show plan while speaking slowly and clearly. Give details about the show's time period, location, and characters. Explain how you think some of the events affected life in the area. Ask your classmates if they have comments to add.

Reflect on Your Project

Think about the work you did in this chapter and on your project. Use the questions below to help guide your thoughts.

1. Why did you select those particular people, events, and location for your Southwest TV show? _____

_____

2. Did you use facts and details to support your conclusions about the events? _____

_____

3. Did you ask your classmates for feedback? _____

_____

Chapter Connections

Use pictures, words, or both to reflect on what you learned in this chapter.

The most interesting thing I learned:

Something I learned from a classmate:

A connection I can make with my own life:

If You Build It, . . .

CHARACTERS

Narrator	Karen	Entire Class
Mr. Roab	Jim	Mary
Mrs. Roab	Teacher	Sam

Narrator: It is 1941 in Salinas, California. We are near a tent in a grove where the Roab family now lives. The Roabs once were farmers in Oklahoma. Then the rains stopped, and a drought set in. Soon the land dried up and their home became part of the Dust Bowl. Without rain, the Roabs could no longer farm. Finally, they were forced to move, and they drove all the way to California. So far, life in California has been hard. The Roabs want their children to go to school and get a good education. However, the Roabs and other migrants struggle just to survive.

Copyright © McGraw-Hill Education
Farm Security Administration/Office of War Information Black-And-White Negatives, Library of Congress, LC-DIG-fsa-8b27115

Narrator: Mrs. Roab calls out to her husband.

Mrs. Roab: It's almost time for lunch!

Karen: Please make lunch for us, too.

Mrs. Roab: Why are you home from school so early?

Karen: It's been a terrible day. The school turned us away.

Jim: They called us "Okies." They said Okies were not welcome in their school.

Mrs. Roab: What are we going to do?

Mr. Roab: I heard about a man named Leo Hart who is starting a school for children of migrants and people like us.

Narrator: That morning, Mr. and Mrs. Roab and their children headed to the new school but saw that there was no school building. Classes were being taught outside.

Mr. Roab: Pardon me. We're looking for the school that Mr. Hart is opening.

Teacher: This is it.

Entire Class: We still have to build it.

Jim: What do you mean "build it"?

Mary: We're building the school with our bare hands.

Teacher: She's right! We don't have a building yet, but we have acres and acres of land.

Entire Class: Mr. Hart thinks that we'll learn while we're working to build the school.

Teacher: Our students will learn skills like laying bricks, plastering, and painting walls. They will even do some plumbing. We'll build for part of the day and then study the rest of the day.

Mr. Roab: Our kids are good workers, but they've grown a little weak from hunger. It takes a lot of energy to build a school.

Teacher: The school is going to have a working farm. We'll have cows and chickens, and we'll grow our own fruits and vegetables to make our own food.

Mrs. Roab: Well, students, we'd better get started. We have a lot of work left to do!

Narrator: The students went to work. Brick by brick, they built the school.

Mary: I need more bricks.

Jim: How many?

Mary: Let me think. This space takes 6 bricks across and 8 bricks high. Hmmm. 6×8 equals 48. I need 48 bricks.

Entire Class: Let's all count out 48 bricks.

Teacher: Kids, it's time for math class.

Narrator: Every day, the students spent time learning to read, write, and do math.

Teacher: You have all done a great job. Mr. Hart had a brilliant idea. What if our school had a science lab?

Entire Class: For science projects?

Teacher: Yes, for research and experiments.

Entire Class: Are we going to build the lab ourselves?

Karen: Look how much we've already accomplished. We can do anything if we put our minds to it!

Teacher: That was exactly what Mr. Hart was hoping you'd say!

Narrator: And so the students began work constructing a science lab.

Karen: I went to the orchard and picked some apples for everyone.

Sam: Thanks. I'm ready for a snack. It's getting hot out here.

Karen: I wish I could dive into a pool and just swim and swim.

Sam: Wouldn't it be great if we had a swimming pool?

Mary: Quit dreaming and get back to work.

Sam: I'm not dreaming. If we can build all of this, why couldn't we build a swimming pool, too?

Entire Class: Let's ask Mr. Hart!

Narrator: Over time, the students built a school, a lab, and a swimming pool. Soon their school became national news. People said it was the best school around. It was all thanks to one man named Leo Hart, who inspired others to make a difference.

Write About It

If you could build your own school, what would you include? Describe everything you would build, and share why you would do it that way.

Chapter 6

The West

What Draws People to the West?

In this chapter, you'll read about early peoples living in the region. You'll read about why and how people from all over the world came to the region. Learning about the region's past will help you understand why people are drawn to the West today.

Talk About It

Discuss with your partner any questions you have. What do you know about the industries, natural resources, and climate in the West? As you research the events and people of the region, look for answers to your questions.

Inquiry Project

Best of the West Documentary

Work with a small team to make a documentary about a group of people who made an important impact in the West. Include fictional interviews with people who lived at the time. Explain in the documentary how these people changed history.

Project Checklist

☐ **Discuss** how to narrow down your project to one group.

☐ **Assign** who will narrate, participate in the interviews, and prepare any visuals.

☐ **Write** a script and create a storyboard to show the flow of the events and people.

☐ **Prepare** visuals, such as photos, maps, or illustrations.

☐ **Rehearse** the performance and readings before presenting it to the class.

My Research Plan

Write down any research questions you have that will help you plan your project. You can add questions as you carry out your research.

_____

_____

_____

_____

_____

_____

Complete this chapter's Word Rater.
Write notes as you learn more about each word.

animation
My Notes
- ☐ Know It!
- ☐ Heard It!
- ☐ Don't Know It!
_____
_____
_____

arid
My Notes
- ☐ Know It!
- ☐ Heard It!
- ☐ Don't Know It!
_____
_____
_____

boomtown
My Notes
- ☐ Know It!
- ☐ Heard It!
- ☐ Don't Know It!
_____
_____
_____

continental divide
My Notes
- ☐ Know It!
- ☐ Heard It!
- ☐ Don't Know It!
_____
_____
_____

deforestation
My Notes
- ☐ Know It!
- ☐ Heard It!
- ☐ Don't Know It!
_____
_____
_____

internment camp

☐ Know It!
☐ Heard It!
☐ Don't Know It!

My Notes

_____

_____

_____

microchip

☐ Know It!
☐ Heard It!
☐ Don't Know It!

My Notes

_____

_____

_____

Pacific Rim

☐ Know It!
☐ Heard It!
☐ Don't Know It!

My Notes

_____

_____

_____

stagecoach

☐ Know It!
☐ Heard It!
☐ Don't Know It!

My Notes

_____

_____

_____

stock market

☐ Know It!
☐ Heard It!
☐ Don't Know It!

My Notes

_____

_____

_____

Lesson 1

What Role Did the Geography of the West Have in Developing Early Cultures?

Lesson Outcomes

What Am I Learning?

In this lesson, you're going to use your investigative skills to explore how the environment of the West influenced the people who first lived there.

Why Am I Learning It?

Reading and talking about the environment of the West will help you learn about the advantages and challenges of the early peoples.

How Will I Know That I Learned It?

You will be able to explain why people lived where they did and the challenges they faced.

Talk About It

COLLABORATE

Look closely at the picture. What does it show? When do you think these people lived? What clues in the picture support your answer?

Small bands of people moved from place to place, following the prehistoric mammals they hunted.

1 Inspect

Read Look at the title. What do you think this text will be about?

- **Circle** the names of the animals in the Yokuts story.
- **Discuss** the role each animal has in the story.

My Notes

_____

_____

_____

_____

_____

_____

_____

_____

_____

_____

_____

_____

_____

_____

_____

Where Do We Come From?

All people wonder how the world began and where people came from. There are different ways to explain events from long ago.

Each Native American culture has stories passed down through the generations. These stories explain how the world began, and how people came into existence. Here is an example from the Yokuts people:

The Beginning of the World - A Yokuts Story

Before there were people, there was only water everywhere. Coyote found a certain diving species of duck and sent one of them to dive down. At first, it said it was unable to. Then it went down. Coyote took the earth from it and sent it for seeds. When the duck brought these, he mixed them with the earth and water, then the mixture swelled until the water had disappeared. The earth was there.

Scientists offer another explanation for how people first came to North America. They think the answer is in a land bridge called Beringia. Beringia connected the continents of Asia and North America ten to twenty thousand years ago. Large glaciers caused the sea level to drop 300 feet, exposing a strip of land between the continents. Animals roamed Beringia and were hunted by people from Asia.

Over time, the glaciers melted, covering the exposed land with water again. The hunters migrated into North America, some traveling as far as South America.

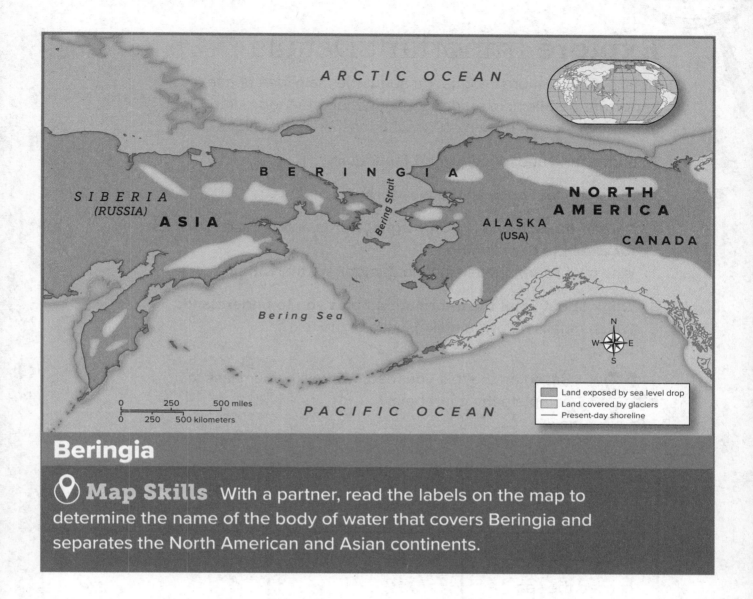

Beringia

Map Skills With a partner, read the labels on the map to determine the name of the body of water that covers Beringia and separates the North American and Asian continents.

2 Find Evidence

Reread Explain what caused early humans to leave Beringia.

Underline Draw a line under details that support your answer.

In your explanation, be sure to describe the effects that glaciers in North America had on the migration of animals and people.

3 Make Connections

Talk Discuss with a partner why some areas of Beringia are different colors. Why is this information included on the map?

Then talk about other information that the map provides that is not in the text.

Explore Important Details

Details provide more information about the main idea of a text. **Important details** help readers to understand the topic. Important details can include examples, descriptions, or explanations.

To understand and identify important details:

1. **Read the text once all the way through.**

2. **Reread the text and look for signal words and phrases such as *for example* or *including*.**
   Why might some details be more important than others?

3. **Think about what the information helps you to understand.**
   Which details help you make sense of the text?

 Based on the text you read, work with your class to complete the chart below.

Important Detail from Text	What It Explains	What It Helps Me Understand
Large glaciers caused the sea level to drop 300 feet, exposing a strip of land between the continents.		

Investigate!

Read pages 302–311 in your Research Companion. Use your investigative skills to identify details about the lives of the early peoples of the West.

Important Detail from the Text	What It Explains	What It Helps Me Understand

Think About It

Review

How would you describe the lives of the early peoples in the West?

Write About It

Write and Cite Evidence

Choose a Native American group that you have read about. Imagine you are a journalist. Write an article describing the daily life of a member of the group you chose.

_____

_____

_____

_____

_____

_____

_____

_____

_____

_____

_____

_____

Talk About It

Compare and Contrast

Share your news article with a partner. Discuss how the lives of the Native American group you chose were similar to and different from your partner's choice. If you and your partner chose the same group, discuss how the lives of men and women in that group were similar and different.

graphy

Connect to the

Pull It Together

What geographic factors drew early peoples to the West?

_____

_____

_____

_____

_____

_____

_____

_____

Inquiry Project Notes

_____

_____

_____

_____

Why Did People in the Past Migrate to the West?

Lesson Outcomes

What Am I Learning?

In this lesson, you're going to use your investigative skills to learn about why people migrated to the West.

Why Am I Learning It?

Reading and talking about why people migrated to the West will help you learn more about different people who helped develop the states in the West.

How Will I Know That I Learned It?

You will be able to explain the different reasons people moved to the West.

Talk About It   COLLABORATE

Look at the picture. What are the people doing? How would this help people who are traveling west?

Most of the workers who built the Transcontinental Railroad were immigrants.

Manifest Destiny

In the early 1800s, people in the United States traveled westward. They wanted to claim land to farm and to build houses. Most of the West was divided into large territories. Some were organized under the Mexican government and some under the United States government. Borders changed frequently and the land was often disputed. Native Americans were already living in all of these territories. To them, the settlers seemed like intruders.

Many Americans believed that it was the *destiny*, or fate, of the United States to occupy all the land between the Atlantic and Pacific Oceans. They believed that this destiny was *manifest*, or obvious. This belief was called Manifest Destiny. People who believed in Manifest Destiny thought that their God meant for them to have that land.

On March 2, 1846, William Gilpin addressed the United States Senate. Gilpin was an advisor to President James K. Polk and a passionate believer in Manifest Destiny. He hoped to win the U.S. Senate members over to the cause. In his speech, he said, "The . . . destiny of the American people is to subdue the continent. . . to animate the many hundred millions of its people, and to cheer them upward—to set the principle of self-government at work. . ."

At this time, the United States did not own land all the way west to the Pacific Ocean. The concept of Manifest Destiny fueled and supported the country as it got control of lands farther and farther west.

1 Inspect

Read Look at the map. What do you think this text will be about?

- **Circle** words you don't know.
- **Underline** clues that help you answer these questions: Why did Americans want to settle in the West? How did this cause conflict with the people living there?
- **Discuss** with a partner what the term "Manifest Destiny" means and what role this concept played in the conflict.

My Notes

_____

_____

_____

_____

_____

_____

_____

_____

_____

_____

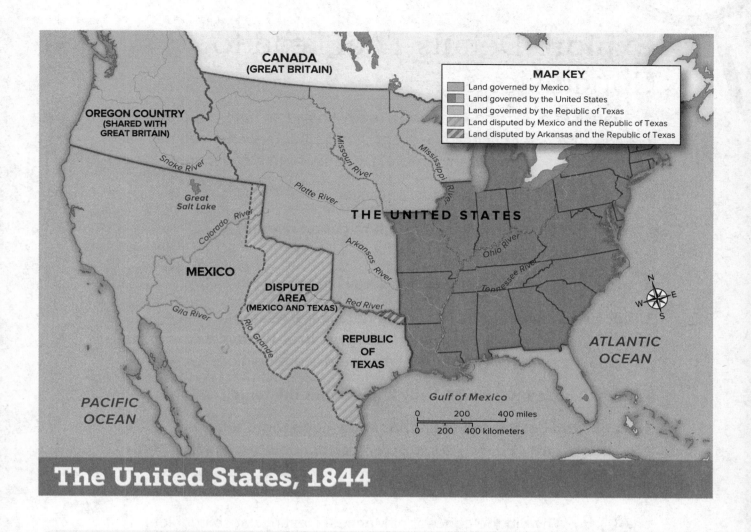

The United States, 1844

MAP KEY
- Land governed by Mexico
- Land governed by the United States
- Land governed by the Republic of Texas
- Land disputed by Mexico and the Republic of Texas
- Land disputed by Arkansas and the Republic of Texas

CANADA (GREAT BRITAIN)

OREGON COUNTRY (SHARED WITH GREAT BRITAIN)

Snake River

Great Salt Lake

Colorado River

MEXICO

Gila River

Rio Grande

DISPUTED AREA (MEXICO AND TEXAS)

Red River

REPUBLIC OF TEXAS

PACIFIC OCEAN

Missouri River

Platte River

Mississippi River

THE UNITED STATES

Arkansas River

Ohio River

Tennessee River

ATLANTIC OCEAN

Gulf of Mexico

0   200   400 miles
0   200   400 kilometers

2 Find Evidence

Reread How do the words of William Gilpin on page 260 help you understand Manifest Destiny? What do you think Gilpin is talking about when he says, "to animate the many hundred millions of its people, and to cheer them upward—to set the principle of self-government at work"?

3 Make Connections

Talk Discuss with a partner why people who believed in Manifest Destiny thought that the United States had a right to take over the western territories.

Discuss reasons other people might have had for disagreeing with Manifest Destiny.

Explore Details That Lead to Conclusions

The **details** in a text and what you already know can help you come to a conclusion. A **conclusion** is a decision or judgment. Sometimes a conclusion is an important idea, fact, or answer to a question.

To find the details that lead to a conclusion:

1. **Read the text all the way through to get an overall understanding.**

2. **Identify the author's important details or ideas.**

3. **Look for ways that the important details are related.**
    Ask yourself, *Why is the author telling me this? What is the point? What details are facts? What details are opinions?*

4. **Think about what you already know about the topic.**

5. **Put all the details and your prior knowledge together.**
    Ask yourself, *What conclusion, or important point, does this information lead up to?*

COLLABORATE
Why did the concept of Manifest Destiny cause conflicts in the West? Based on the text you read, work with your class to complete the diagram below.

Details
I. Many Americans believed that it was the destiny, or fate, of the United States to occupy the land between the Atlantic and Pacific Oceans.
2.

Conclusion

Investigate!

Read pages 312–321 in your Research Companion. Use your investigative skills to look for text evidence that supports the conclusion that is drawn from the text.

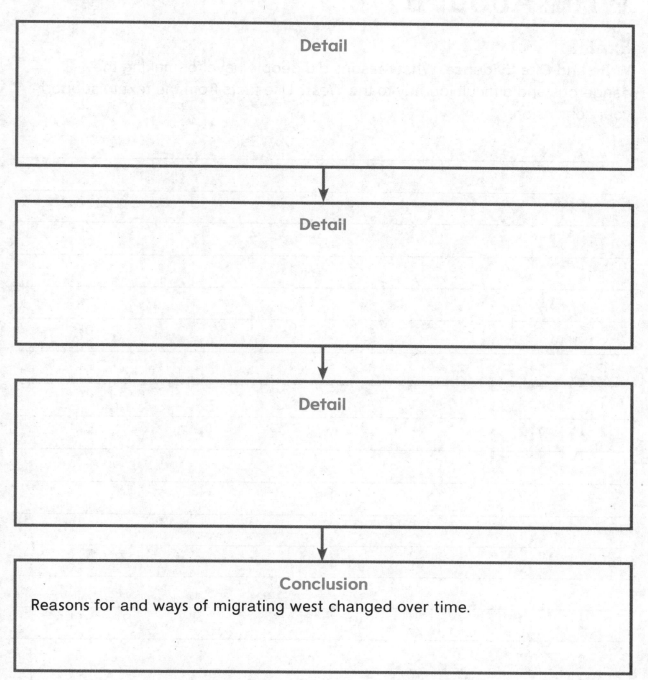

Detail

Detail

Detail

Conclusion

Reasons for and ways of migrating west changed over time.

Think About It

Review

Based on the information you have gathered, why were people willing to face dangers to move to the West?

Write About It

Explain

Write and Cite Evidence What reasons did people have for making the dangerous and difficult journey to the West? Use facts from the text to support your conclusion.

_____

_____

_____

_____

_____

_____

_____

_____

_____

_____

_____

_____

_____

_____

Talk About It

Draw Conclusions

Share your response with a partner. Together discuss why, despite all the danger, many people still decided to move to the West.

Connect to the

Pull It Together

Now that you know some reasons people moved to the West in the 1800s, do you think those reasons might be the same or different today? Do they face the same challenges today? Give examples for your answers.

_____

_____

_____

_____

_____

_____

_____

Inquiry Project Notes

_____

_____

_____

_____

_____

How Have People Reacted to Changes and Challenges in the West?

Lesson Outcomes

What Am I Learning?

In this lesson, you're going to use your investigative skills to learn how people reacted to changes and challenges in the West.

Why Am I Learning It?

Reading and talking about the reactions people had to the changes and challenges of the times will help you learn more about the West today.

How Will I Know That I Learned It?

You will be able to explain how important people and events changed the lives of people in the West.

Talk About It

COLLABORATE

Look closely at the photograph. What signs of the bombing can you see? Why do you think the United States entered World War II after this attack?

On December 7, 1941, the Japanese bombed the U.S. Naval Base at Pearl Harbor in Hawaii.

Pearl Harbor, Hawaii

Read Look at the title. What do you think the primary source—and the text on this page—is about?

- **Circle** words you don't know.
- **Underline** clues that help you answer these questions:
  - What was attacked?
  - Why was the attack important?
  - What were the results of the attack?
- **Discuss** with a partner what Corporal Nightingale saw and heard.

My Notes

_____

_____

_____

_____

_____

_____

_____

_____

_____

The Attack at Pearl Harbor

World War II started in 1939. Countries around the world joined the Axis powers or the Allies, or Allied nations. For two years, the United States did not join one side or the other. Then, on December 7, 1941, Japanese warplanes attacked the U.S. naval base at Pearl Harbor. A naval base provides a place for vessels such as ships and submarines to anchor. It also offers support for the vessels, equipment, and the soldiers.

About 2,400 Americans were killed and 1,200 were wounded in the attack. The Pacific Fleet was severely damaged. The naval base lost battleships, destroyers, and planes. Japan was part of the Axis, so as a result of the attack, the United States joined the Allied nations to fight the war.

Factories in the United States produced weapons, ships, and planes to supply the armed forces. Many people went to fight the war. New workers stepped up to replace them, including women. The Great Depression had caused a shortage of jobs. Now people could find work in the factories.

When the attack on Pearl Harbor began, Marine Corporal E.C. Nightingale was aboard the USS *Arizona*, one of the battleships docked there. His words help us understand what happened on that morning.

In Their Words . . .
Marine Corporal E.C. Nightingale

"At approximately eight o'clock on the morning of December 7, 1941, I was leaving the breakfast table when the ship's siren for air defense sounded. . . . Suddenly I heard an explosion. I ran to the port door leading to the quarterdeck and saw a bomb strike a barge of some sort alongside the NEVADA, or in that vicinity. The marine color guard came in at this point saying we were being attacked. I could distinctly hear machine gun fire. I believe at this point our anti-aircraft battery opened up.

". . . I started for my battle station. . . . The men seemed extremely calm and collected. I reached the boat deck and our anti-aircraft guns were in full action, firing very rapidly . . . [w]hen it seemed a bomb struck our quarterdeck. I could hear shrapnel or fragments whistling past me. . . .

"I had only been there a short time when a terrible explosion caused the ship to shake violently. I looked at the boat deck, and everything seemed aflame forward of the mainmast . . . [t]he Major ordered us to leave."

—excerpt from *Pearl Harbor: Why, How, Fleet Salvage and Final Appraisal* (1968)

2 Find Evidence

Reread How does Marine Corporal Nightingale's account of the attack help you understand how the attack affected the naval base?

Reread the words, "everything seemed aflame." What do these words mean to you?

3 Make Connections

Talk Discuss with a partner the results of the attack on Pearl Harbor. How did America's joining the war affect the number of jobs in the United States?

How and why did the workforce in the United States change?

Explore Compare and Contrast

Authors often write to **compare** (to show how things are the same or similar) or to **contrast** (to show how things are different).

To compare and contrast:

1. **Read the text once all the way through.**
   This will help you understand what the text is about.

2. **Reread the text. Make sure you understand the most important details.**
   What words or sentences stand out to you as being important?

3. **Look for differences in a topic.**
   For example, how did the types of goods manufactured in the United States change after the United States went to war?

4. **Look for similarities in a topic.**
   For example, what industries played a part in the economy both before and after the war?

Based on the text you read, work with your class to complete the chart below. Compare and contrast life in the United States before and after a specific event.

Event	Life Before	Life After
On December 7, 1941, Japan attacked Pearl Harbor.		

Investigate!

Read pages 322–331 in your Research Companion. Use your investigative skills to look for text evidence that helps you compare and contrast life in the United States before and after specific events. This chart will help you organize your notes.

Event	Life Before	Life After
In the mid- to late-1800s, many people moved west and the population grew.		
In 1882, Congress passed the Chinese Exclusion Act and the Geary Act in 1892.		

Report Your Findings

Think About It

Compare

Review your research. Based on the information you have gathered, how did different groups of Americans live and work together during World War II?

Write About It

Recall

What event led to the United States entering World War II?
Why was that significant?

_____

_____

_____

_____

_____

Write and Cite Evidence

How did lives change for different groups of people in the United States during World War II? Use facts from the texts to explain your response.

_____

_____

_____

_____

_____

_____

Talk About It

Explain

With a partner, discuss how major events changed how diverse groups of people lived and worked together in the West.

Connect to the

Pull It Together

Think about the changes and challenges people in the West have faced. Tell how one of them helped draw people to the West.

_____

_____

_____

_____

_____

_____

Inquiry Project Notes

_____

_____

_____

_____

Lesson 4

How Do Natural Resources Drive the Economy of the West?

Lesson Outcomes

What Am I Learning?

In this lesson, you're going to use your investigative skills to explore the West's natural resources and their impact on the economy.

Why Am I Learning It?

Reading and talking about the West's natural resources help us to learn how they affect its economy.

How Will I Know That I Learned It?

You will be able to identify the West's many natural resources and explain how they impact the region's economy.

Talk About It

COLLABORATE

Look closely at the picture. What natural resources do you see? What resources are missing?

Death Valley, located in West, is the hottest and driest place in North America.

1 Inspect

- **Recall** Look at the heading and the photo. What do you already know about mountains in the West?
- **Underline** the states where the mountains are located.
- **Highlight** the definition of a rain shadow.

My Notes

The West: Mountains and Majesty

The Rocky Mountains are one of the West's best-known features. This chain of tall, rugged mountains extends south from Alaska into the continental United States for more than 3,000 miles. It varies in width from 70 to 300 miles. The Rockies help create short summers and long, cold winters in Alaska. High elevations make for sudden strong storms and deep snow packs.

Two other north-south ranges are located west of the Rocky Mountains. The Cascades are mainly in Washington and Oregon. The Sierra Nevada mountains run through northern and central California. These ranges cut off the cool, wet air that comes from the Pacific Ocean. Rain and snow fall mainly on the western sides of these mountains. The eastern sides are drier and warmer because there is little moisture remaining in the air. This phenomenon is known as a rain shadow. The Great Basin, a low-lying area of land, lies between the Rocky Mountains and the Sierra Nevada and the Cascades. The land here is **arid**, or very dry, and there are few plants.

PRIMARY SOURCE

In Their Words ... Isabella Bird

"The Rocky Mountains realize--nay, exceed--the dream of my childhood. It is magnificent, and the air is lifegiving."

—Isabella Bird, English Traveler, 1873

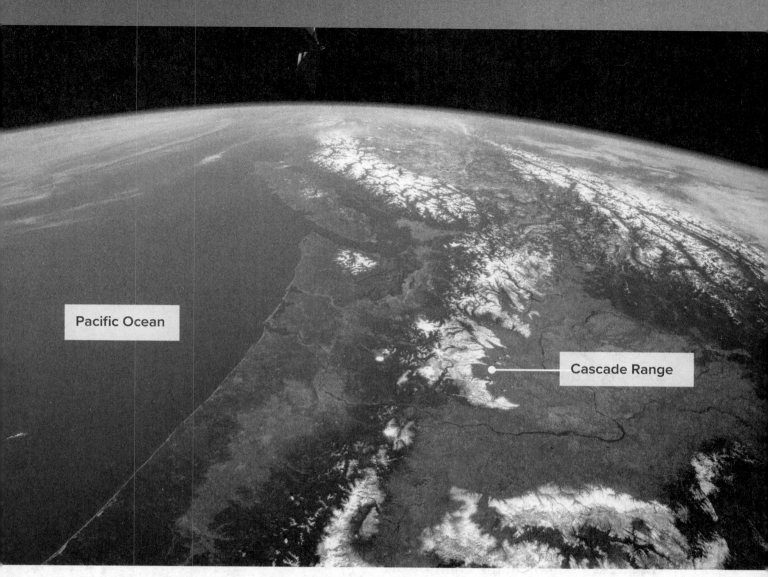

Pacific Ocean

Cascade Range

The rain shadow of a mountain range lies to the east of the range.

2 Find Evidence

Summarize How do mountains impact the West?

Underline the length and width of the Rocky Mountains.

3 Make Connections

Write Look at the photo. Where are the wetter areas of land? Where are the arid regions? How do you know?

Explore Cause and Effect

The **effect** is what happened. The **cause** is why it happened.
To find the cause and effect:

1. **Read the text from beginning to end.**
   This gives you a complete overview of the material and helps
   you understand what the text is about.

2. **Reread the text and look for ideas that tell you
   what happened.**
   What occurred because of something else? The result is the
   effect.

3. **Reread the text and look for a detail that tells you why
   it happened.**
   What occurred that led to the effect? This is the cause.

4. **Ask yourself, "What is the relationship between the cause and
   the effect?"**
   How did one event lead to another?

COLLABORATE
Based on the text you read, work with your class to
complete the chart below.

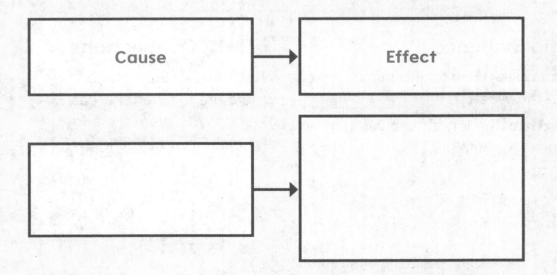

Investigate!

Read pages 332–341 in your Research Companion. Use your investigative skills to look for text evidence that tells you what happened and why it happened. This chart will help you organize your notes.

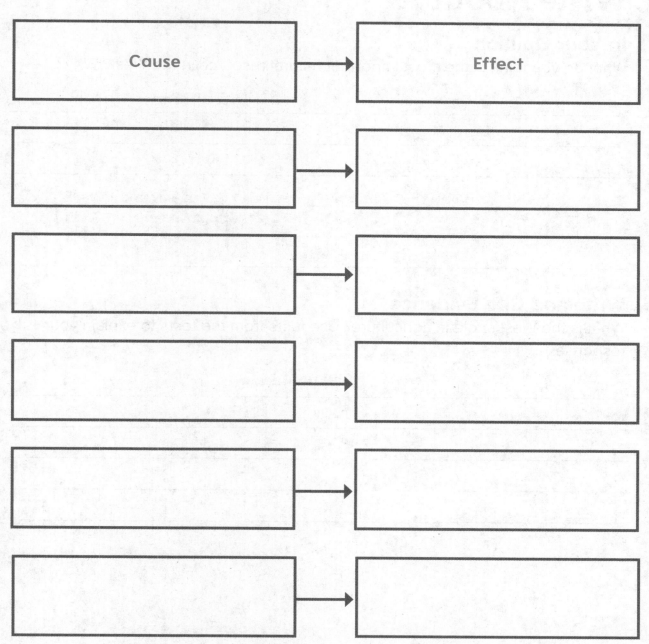

Cause → Effect

Think About It

Review

Based on the information you have gathered, what are some similarities states in the West share? What are some differences between them?

Write About It

In Your Opinion

What do you think is the most important natural resource in the West? Why?

_____

_____

_____

_____

_____

_____

Write and Cite Evidence

What is the West's role in agriculture? Use facts from the texts to explain your response.

_____

_____

_____

_____

_____

Talk About It

Explain

With a partner, talk about water in the West. How is water brought to drier areas in the region?

 eography

Connect to the

Summarize

How do natural resources drive people to the West?

_____

_____

_____

_____

_____

_____

_____

_____

Inquiry Project Notes

_____

_____

_____

_____

_____

Lesson 5

What Makes the West a Worldwide Success?

Lesson Outcomes

What Am I Learning?

In this lesson, you're going to use your investigative skills to explore how activities and industries the West have experienced success, both at home and around the world.

Why Am I Learning It?

Reading and talking about the West's activities and industries helps you to see how it fits into the economy of the United States and the rest of the world.

How Will I Know That I Learned It?

You will be able to explain the West's contributions to entertainment, computer technology, and trade.

Talk About It

COLLABORATE

Look at the picture. In what ways is the West connected to the rest of the world?

The Port of Seattle is a major trade hub of the West.

Trade and the West

International trade is an important part of the West's economy. All over the world, people buy products that come from western states. Computers and electronic products, transportation equipment, chemicals, machinery, and food are some of the categories of items western states export. Other products include primary metals mined from natural sources, nonmetallic minerals, and petroleum and coal products.

Mexico and Canada are significant trading partners with states in the West. Many western states border these countries. Because many states in the West are on the coast of the Pacific Ocean, it is also easy to trade with companies from the Pacific Basin. These countries include China, Japan, South Korea, Hong Kong, and Taiwan.

States along the west coast have many ports that both receive and send container ships around the world. The busiest ports include Los Angeles, Long Beach, and Oakland in California. Seattle-Tacoma in Washington handles more than 5 percent of the U.S. market. Anchorage, Alaska, connects frequently with markets in Asia. Expanding trade has helped the port cities grow and become thriving centers of business and culture.

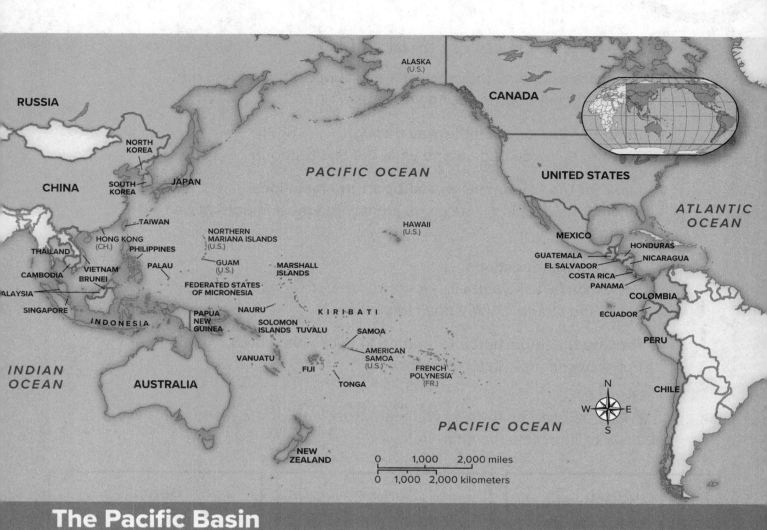

The Pacific Basin

2 Find Evidence

Locate Why is the West in a good position to trade internationally?

Underline the products that western states export.

3 Make Connections

Write What other regions in the United States have busy ports for international trade?

Explore Summarizing

To **summarize**, identify the main idea and supporting details and then retell them briefly in your own words.

1. **Read the text once all the way through.**
    This will help you understand what the text is about.

2. **Look for the key details that support the main idea.**
    Finding the details will help you identify the most important part of the text.

3. **Ask yourself questions.**
    For example, ask yourself, *"How can I restate what the author wants me to know? Why does this matter?"*

4. **Restate the important information in your own words.**
    Put your summary in the bottom box.

 Based on the text you read, work with your class to complete the chart below.

Detail:	Detail:	Detail:
International trade allows people worldwide to buy products from the West.		

Summary:

Investigate!

Read pages 342–349 in your Research Companion. Use your investigative skills to summarize the text. This chart will help you organize your notes.

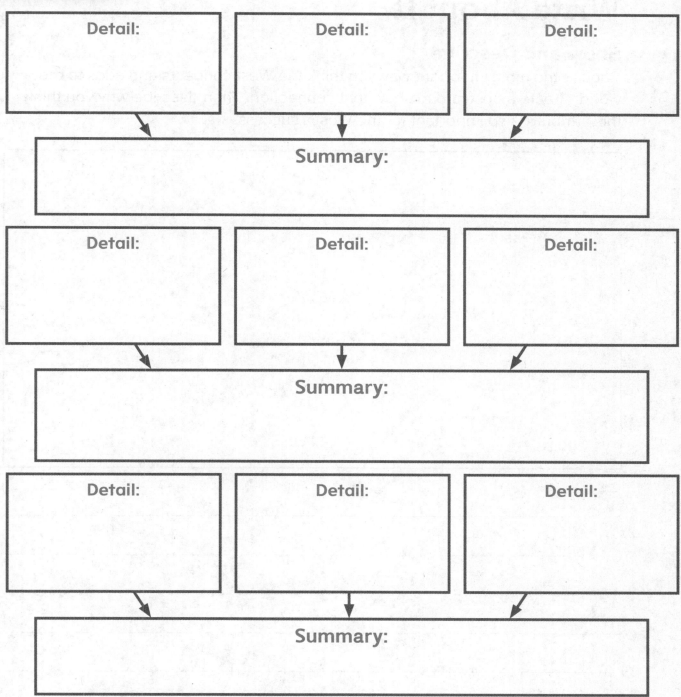

Detail:

Detail:

Detail:

Summary:

Detail:

Detail:

Detail:

Summary:

Detail:

Detail:

Detail:

Summary:

Think About It

Review your research

Based on the information you have gathered, what makes the West a worldwide success? What are the different ways the West connects with the world?

Write About It

Show and Describe

Choose the most important way you think the West connects and adds to the world. Create a postcard to show that connection. Then describe why you think this attribute is so important for the West's success.

Talk About It

Explain Share your postcard and explanation with a partner. Discuss why you made your choice.

nomics

Connect to the

Analyze
How do the West's connections to the world help draw people to the region?

_____

_____

_____

_____

_____

_____

 Inquiry Project Notes

_____

_____

_____

_____

_____

_____

What Draws People to the West?

Inquiry Project

Best of the West Documentary

Now complete your Best of the West Documentary project with a checklist, and then present it to your class.

Complete Your Project

Use this checklist to evaluate your project. If you left anything out, here's your chance to fix it!

- ☐ Write a strong beginning and ending to tie all the information together.

- ☐ Check that your documentary has accurate facts.

- ☐ Provide a brief outline to your group that assigns each member's role during the presentation.

- ☐ Practice giving the presentation. Edit and adjust any scenes for a better flow.

Share Your Project

Now's the time for your small group to present your project to the class. Introduce your topic while speaking slowly and loudly. Make eye contact with the class. Display visuals so that all can see them. Ask your classmates if they have any questions.

Reflect on Your Project

Think about the work you did in this chapter and on your project. Use the questions below to help guide your thoughts.

1. Why did you select the topic of your project?

_____

2. Did you use interesting facts and details that your classmates may not know? _____

_____

3. Did you ask your classmates for feedback? _____

_____

Chapter Connections

Use pictures, words, or both to reflect on what you learned in this chapter.

The most interesting thing I learned:

Something I learned from a classmate:

A connection I can make with my own life:

Reference Source

The Reference Section has a glossary of vocabulary words from the chapters in this book. Use this section to explore new vocabulary as you investigate and take action.

Glossary

A

abolitionist a person who wants to stop or end slavery

aerospace the Earth's atmosphere and the space beyond

alternative energy energy produced from a renewable resource that creates little or no pollution

amendment a change in wording or meaning especially in a law, bill, or motion

animation a method of arranging filmed images to create the effect of movement

annex to attach as an addition

arid very dry

arroyo a creek in a dry region

assembly line an arrangement of machines, equipment, and workers in which work passes from operation to operation in a direct line until the product is made

automation the method of making a device, a process, or a system operate by itself

B

boomtown a town that builds up quickly around an industry or economic opportunity

boycott a refusal to buy a certain product to bring attention to a problem

butte a hill with steep sides standing in a flat area

C

charter a document granting someone special legal powers

colonist a person who takes part in founding a settlement or territory

commerce buying and selling of goods especially on a large scale and between different places

continental divide the line of highest points of land separating the waters flowing west from those flowing north or east

D

deforestation the action or process of clearing an area of forests

democracy a form of government that is run by its people

discrimination the act of treating a person or a group unfairly by other people or groups

drainage a system used to remove water or liquid waste

E

estuary the place where fresh water from a river mixes with the salt water from an ocean

ethnic of or relating to groups of people with common traits and customs and a sense of shared identity

evacuate to remove people from a place of danger

expansion the act of becoming larger

expedition a journey or trip undertaken for a specific purpose

experiment a procedure carried out under controlled conditions in order to discover something

G

geometric using straight or curved lines in designs or outlines

I

immigrant a person who moves from one country to live in another

import something brought into a country

industrialization the widespread development of manufacturing or production in a region, country, or culture

internment camp *Internment* means putting a person in prison or other kinds of detention, generally in wartime. During World War II, the American government sent many Japanese Americans to internment camps, fearing that they might be loyal to Japan.

interstate a system of highways that connects cities and states

invasive tending to spread

irrigation the use of canals, ditches, and pipes to bring water to dry land

L

latitude an imaginary line of distance north or south of the Equator measured in degrees

longitude an imaginary line of distance east or west of the Prime Meridian measured in degrees

M

microchip a tiny computer part that allows a computer to make calculations

mission a religious settlement or church

N

negotiate to have a discussion with another so as to arrive at an agreement

P

Pacific Rim the countries bordering on or located in the Pacific Ocean

plantation an agricultural estate

prairie a large area of level or rolling grassland

presidio a fortified military outpost or fort

protest to object strongly

proximity the state or condition of being near

Q

quarry an open pit usually for obtaining building stone, slate, or limestone

R

raw material natural or processed physical matter that can be converted into a new and useful product

reservation an area of public land set aside for a specific purpose

revolutionary being or bringing about a big or important change

rural of or relating to the country, country people or life, or agriculture

scarcity a very small supply

secede to withdraw from an organization

sharecropper a farmer who works land for the owner and receives part of the value of what is harvested, rather than receiving a standard wage

sovereign politically independent

stagecoach a vehicle pulled by horses that carries passengers and mail

stock market an area of economic activity in which stocks, or financial shares of ownership in a corporation, are bought, sold, and traded

suffrage the right to vote

waterway a body of water through which ships can travel

Y

yeoman a small landowning farmer